Meaningful Mentoring

A Handbook of Effective Strategies, Projects and Activities

Helping You Become a Co-Pilot in an
Adolescent's Life (Grades 6-12)

by Robert P. Bowman, Ph.D. & Susan C. Bowman, Ed.S.

© 2005, 1997 by
YouthLight, Inc.
Chapin, SC 29036

Meaningful Mentoring Handbook was formally printed as
"Becoming a Co-Pilot: Handbook for Mentors of Adolescents."

Cover Illustration by Sandra Shelton
Layout & Design by Andover Graphics and Elizabeth Madden
Project Editing by Rebecca VanGilder

ISBN 1-889636-05-3

10 9 8 7 6 5 4 3
Printed in the United States of America

Dedication

To our three daughters April, Melissa, and Autumn, and grandson Calvin, whom we hope will become mentors themselves, someday.

Acknowledgments

We would like to thank the following people for their contributions to our books:

Rebecca VanGilder, Lisa Nordlund and Melissa White proofread the manuscripts and contributed to the readability of the books.

The following people provided reviews of the program and provided many valuable suggestions:

- Arlonial Bradford-Jackson
- Josh Lorick
- Lollie Becton
- Norma Colwell
- Ron Miles

Julie Chibarro reviewed the program and provided us with supplemental articles for our review of the literature on mentoring.

The following students from Newberry High School (SC) were the first to participate in the Co-Piloting program. Their suggestions helped us to ensure that the handouts were useful and easy to understand.

- Leitha Bundrick
- Amy Davis
- Sharee Graham
- Natalia Jackson
- Carly Lester
- Kizzy Maitland
- Rashida Porter
- Larry Pratt Jr.
- Robert Rivera
- Karisha Walker
- Sabrina Walker

In addition, thanks to middle school students Mara Ahmadi and Jennifer Stewart who reviewed selected activities in the handbook and provided valuable input.

We would also like to thank all the professionals we met during seminars and conferences we conducted around the United States during the past nine years. We learned much from the hundreds of people who tried out parts of our mentoring program, and sent us information or told us about their programs.

Lastly, we would like to thank God for being our foremost mentor. Without His guidance and blessings, this work would not have been completed.

Table of Contents

Chapter 1

Building a Foundation

"A hundred years from now it will not matter what my bank account was, the sort of house I lived in, or the kind of car I drove...

But the world may be different because I was important in the life of a child."

Author Unknown

Building a Foundation

Most people remember with fondness at least one person who had a special, positive impact on their life. This "influencer" was most likely someone who gave them extra attention and encouragement, and communicated a deep belief in their potential.

Unfortunately, many disadvantaged young people will not find such a positive influencer by chance. This is why the Co-Piloting Mentor Program was developed. This program provides trained mentors (Co-Pilots) for young people (Pilots) who need extra support and encouragement in their lives. These Pilots can be as young as pre-kindergartners and as old as 12th graders.

What is a Co-Pilot?

A Co-Pilot is a volunteer mentor to a needy adolescent. He/she works to provide this young person with a special, encouraging relationship that will hopefully become a foundation for success in that adolescent's life. Through this relationship, a Co-Pilot attempts to foster the young person's self-worth, success-motivation, coping skills, and character strengths. The Co-Piloting program provides specialized training and other kinds of support to help ensure that this mentoring relationship will be a positive experience for both mentor and adolescent.

Real co-pilots receive <u>specialized</u> training. They learn a particular set of skills and procedures, and develop a clear understanding of their responsibilities. They also learn that they are not ultimately in command of the flight; that's the pilot's job. In addition, they learn how to provide crucial background assistance for the pilot, providing navigation and trouble-shooting, if needed.

Similarly, a Co-Pilot mentor learns a specialized set of skills and procedures to become an encourager, navigator, and back-up flyer to his/her pilot (adolescent). Ultimately, a Co-Pilot mentor works to help a disadvantaged young person learn how to take flight and soar to new heights in his/her life.

Who Needs a Co-Pilot?

Many disadvantaged adolescents do not have positive role models in their lives. Instead, they are constantly bombarded by various media with examples of negative heroes who they come to idolize. These teens also tend to admire older juveniles or young adults who may "hang out" near their homes or who are friends with their older siblings. Without opportunities to meet and work with encouraging mentors, these youths are likely to follow the same negative life styles they see around them each day.

4

Some young people do not realize that they continue to be worthwhile and capable, regardless of discouraging or hurtful events they may have experienced. Some of these youths, for example, enter a cycle of failure as a result of repeatedly receiving failing grades in school. These experiences lead to even more frustration and discouragement. Without a strong, encouraging person in their lives, these adolescents may eventually turn to thrill-seeking, intoxicants, alcohol/drugs, and/or other means of escape. Through such escapism, they may be vainly attempting to relieve the pain that accompanies the most disabling feeling of all . . . a sense of hopelessness.

In contrast, other adolescents feel super-human as if invincible to negative consequences. Without a positive person in their lives who can help them explore realistic consequences, these young people may come to believe that they are indestructible. They may use self-talk to convince themselves that, regardless of what they do, they won't get "busted," hurt, addicted, pregnant, or diseased. The consequences of this kind of attitude have become much more deadly in recent years.

There are many problems that affect today's youth. Talking about these difficulties is a favorite pastime among many adults. Congratulations! You have decided to go beyond talking and actually take some action to help one of these young people. By volunteering for this program, you are beginning a process that has the potential to change a young person's life.

What is the "Right Stuff" That Makes an Effective Co-Pilot?

Becoming an effective Co-Pilot is not an easy task. You may face challenges from time to time. Navigating through turbulent times with your young Pilot will require you to use many of the abilities you already have and the strategies you will learn from this program.

Co-Piloting is not, however, just about working with your adolescent's difficulties. Often the benefits are mutual for you and the young person. Relating in a playful, encouraging manner with your adolescent will provide you both with many fun and personally uplifting experiences. Your work with your Pilot will provide you both with many joyful and meaningful experiences.

An effective Co-Pilot is someone who has the skill, ability, and commitment to help bring about positive changes in a needy young person's life. First and foremost, your Pilot must come to see that you possess and display certain personal characteristics. The following activity will help you explore these qualities which are the foundation of effective mentoring.

Activity 1.1: Think of a Mentor

Directions: As you grew up, there were probably several people who had positive influences on your life. However, some of these people influenced you more than others.

Think of a positive mentor you once had. Perhaps it was someone older than you whom you admired and tried to emulate. On the lines below, write some of the positive qualities that this person exhibited.

_____   _____

_____   _____

_____   _____

Co-Pilot Characteristics

There are many qualities that distinguish mentors from other people who are less effective influencers. Look through the following seven qualities and compare them to your list. If you have time, discuss each of these characteristics with other Co-Pilots.

Caring

The Co-Pilot has a deep regard for the value and dignity of the Pilot.

Outgoing

The Co-Pilot is friendly, fun loving, and approachable.

Persistent

The Co-Pilot is committed to persevere during rough times.

Insightful

The Co-Pilot is sensitive to the Pilot's cultural, gender, and religious perspectives.

Link

The Co-Pilot connects the Pilot with outside resources when needed.

Open-Minded

The Co-Pilot shows acceptance of the Pilot's worth and potential, regardless of his/her past actions.

Trustworthy

The Co-Pilot shows that he/she is dependable and genuine.

Co-Piloting Roles

To be effective with your Pilot, you will need to continually demonstrate these "Co-Pilot Characteristics." The following are ways that you can show these characteristics to your Pilot.

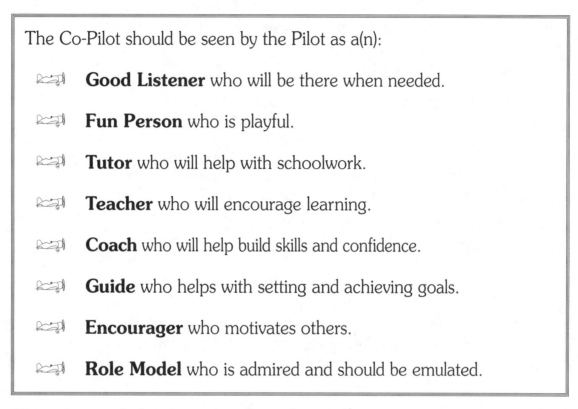

The Co-Pilot should be seen by the Pilot as a(n):

- **Good Listener** who will be there when needed.

- **Fun Person** who is playful.

- **Tutor** who will help with schoolwork.

- **Teacher** who will encourage learning.

- **Coach** who will help build skills and confidence.

- **Guide** who helps with setting and achieving goals.

- **Encourager** who motivates others.

- **Role Model** who is admired and should be emulated.

Through your dedication to assuming these roles, your young Pilot will benefit in many ways. Your special support and encouragement will help your Pilot develop feelings of self-worth and self-confidence.

Activity 1.2: Ground Rules for Co-Pilots

Directions: Pair up with another Co-Pilot or join with a small group of participants. Then, discuss one of the ground rules from the following list. In particular, talk about the importance of the rule and what each Co-Pilot should do to ensure that the rule will be followed. When finished, have a representative of your group present a summary of their discussion to the other Co-Pilots.

1. **Confidentiality:** Even with the youngest Pilot, keep specific information that he/she tells you in confidence unless:
   a. Your Pilot has given you permission, or
   b. There is evidence of danger to your Pilot or others. Then, you must tell the Program Coordinator and/or someone to whom you have been directed to refer such cases.

2. **Charity:** Do not become a "Santa Claus" to your Pilot. Too much emphasis on material gifts will work against the development of a healthy mentoring relationship. It is okay, however, to purchase some inexpensive items for your Pilot like incentives, greeting cards, small gifts, or a portfolio cover.

3. **School Policy:** If you are planning to meet your Pilot at school, you must be aware of and follow any school policies that might apply to your work with a student.

4. **Outside Meetings:** If you are planning to meet with your Pilot anywhere other than the school setting, you must first make your Program Coordinator aware and acquire parental/guardian permission.

5. **Commitments:** You must keep your commitments to your Pilot. Too many missed appointments can lead to initial feelings of discouragement and eventually lead to feelings of abandonment in a young person.

6. **Support Group Meetings:** You must attend your Co-Pilot Support Group Meetings. These meetings will provide you and other Co-Pilots with opportunities to share ideas and concerns with each other.

7. **Role Modeling:** Each time you meet with your Pilot, remember to show the seven Co-Pilot Characteristics described earlier in this chapter.

8. **Self-Preservation:** Make sure you take care of yourself and have many enjoyable times with your Pilot.

Activity 1.3: Three Co-Piloting Stories

Directions: In the Appendix on pages 149-154, three people tell of their experiences as Co-Pilots. Reading and comparing these stories will help you develop a more personalized understanding of what some other Co-Pilots have experienced in their programs.

Note that each of the three stories is told by a Co-Pilot from a different kind of program. In "Anna's Story" the Co-Pilot is a teacher. In "Arthur's Story" the Co-Pilot is a bank employee. In "Josh's Story" the Co-Pilot is a senior in high school.

Discussion Questions:
After reading all three Co-Piloting stories, discuss your answers to each of the following questions.

1. What experiences did the three Co-Pilots have that were most similar to each other?

2. What approaches did the Co-Pilots feel were the most effective in helping their Pilots?

3. What do you believe is the most important role a Co-Pilot can play for a young person?

Chapter 2

Relationship-Building Tactics

"Real unselfishness consists in sharing the interests of others."

George Santayana

Relationship-Building Tactics

As a Co-Pilot, you should not think of mentoring as merely looking for your young person's problems and then working to resolve them. The single most important thing that you can do for your Pilot is to provide him/her with a special, positive relationship that will be remembered for a lifetime.

This special relationship will help your adolescent discover many positive things about him/herself. During your meetings, as you provide recurring attention and encouragement, your Pilot will begin to build on his/her self-worth and confidence.

However, realistically there is no guarantee that a close Pilot/Co-Pilot relationship will develop between you and your person. Even if you seem to "hit it off" with your Pilot at the beginning, you may later face challenges in your relationship. Sometimes you may need to be very patient and use every encouraging skill that you can think of. In time, your Pilot will learn to become more comfortable with you and to trust in your helping efforts.

In the previous chapter, we covered the characteristics of an effective Co-Pilot. Now, let's look at the keys to using these characteristics to build an encouraging relationship with your Pilot.

Four Keys to Start a Mentoring Relationship

🔑 1. Listen Attentively

🔑 2. Ask Inviting Questions

🔑 3. Summarize Content and Feeling

🔑 4. Use Strategic Self-Disclosures

1. Listen Attentively

One of the greatest gifts someone can give to a young person is to patiently listen in a deeply caring manner. We may seek out a good listener for ourselves when we have experiences we want to share. Unfortunately, good listeners are difficult to find in today's fast-paced world. Some people don't even take time to carefully and patiently listen to the feelings of their own family members.

Young people become excited when someone encourages them to talk about their interests, concerns, and views of events. For young people to develop positive beliefs about their self-worth, they need a person to show a special interest in them. This means having someone in their lives who will take the time periodically to be an encouraging listener.

As you begin your relationship with your Pilot, you should work especially hard to be a good listener. Attentive listening begins by displaying open and inviting body language to the adolescent. As your Pilot talks to you:

✈️ **Don't** cross your arms, lean too far back, fidget with something in your hands, or look away very often from your Pilot's face.

✈️ **Do** sit with an open, calm posture. Laugh with him/her and keep a facial expression that shows genuine interest in what he/she is saying or doing.

Activity 2.1: Inviting and Uninviting Body Language

Directions: Pair up with another participant and decide who will be the first "Talker." The other person will be the "Listener."

Sit directly facing one another. The Talker should begin by telling about something that happened to him/her during the past month.

At first, the Listener should display positive or "inviting" body language to show he/she is listening attentively. After about 15 seconds, the Listener should start to appear increasingly distracted by:
- Crossing his/her arms and leaning back.
- Looking away from the Talker's face, perhaps staring at his/her watch, then glancing at others in the room.
- Stretching and yawning.
- Using other creative ideas to show as much distraction as possible.

After two minutes, stop and discuss what happened. Then, start the activity again, but this time the same Listener should try to show the Co-Piloting Characteristics through inviting body language. Use the same topic and allow enough time for the Talker to finish his/her story.

Once you and your partner have each had a turn being inviting and uninviting listeners, discuss your answers to the following questions.

Discussion Questions:

1. As a talker, what was it like trying to tell your story to such an uninviting listener? How did this differ when the person became an inviting listener?

2. What are some common mistakes adults make when listening to adolescents?

3. How can you "listen" to your Pilot if he/she is not talkative?

2. Ask Inviting Questions

Asking adolescents questions can make them feel that you are interested in learning more about them and what they are doing. However, some ways of asking questions are clearly better than others. When working with your young Pilot, remember the following hints:

Limit Your Number of Questions: Too many questions can cause a teenager to feel uncomfortable. He/she may begin to wonder why you want to know so much and what you will be doing with the information.

Avoid "Why" Questions: Questions that begin with "Why" can arouse a teen's defenses because it may sound like you are making an accusation. For example, "Why do you feel that way?" is risky to ask an adolescent. A better way to ask this question would be, "What happened that bothered you so much?"

Use "What" or "How" Questions: The most inviting questions for adolescents usually begin with the words, "What" or "How." Though there are many other ways to construct questions, these are usually the most inviting.

The following are examples of inviting "What" and "How" questions for adolescents:

- What is your favorite thing to do in school?

- How would you change school, if you could?

- What do you look for in a friend?

- What do you like to do with your friends?

- How do you deal with stress?

- What do you hope to be doing in five years?

- How are you going to get there?

Activity 2.2: *Reword the Questions*

Directions: Read each of these questions. Then in the space that follows, reword the question using a more inviting "What" or "How" question.

1. Why don't you like school?

2. Are you going to do better next time?

3. Did you work things out with Stephen?

4. Can you tell me about it?

5. Why do you feel that way?

Follow-Up:

Have one person in your Co-Pilot group tell a brief description of something that happened to him/her during the past week. When the story is finished, brainstorm several possible "What" and "How" questions that could be asked. Be sure that the questions follow the story and do not lead the person away from what was said. Remember, a good question "follows the talker's lead" and demonstrates that you are interested in what he/she is saying.

3. Summarize Content and Feeling

An even more intensive tactic that will help strengthen your relationship with your Pilot is summarizing content and feeling. That is, when your Pilot talks or does something, occasionally say something that summarizes what the adolescent said or did.

Becoming comfortable with this kind of statement may take some practice if you have never learned it before. When done accurately and in a caring manner, a summary statement can be very powerful. It sends the message that you are interested in your Pilot and want him/her to continue talking.

Summarizing Content

To summarize content, simply listen to and watch your Pilot for awhile. Then periodically make brief statements (not questions) that tell the essence of what he/she is saying or showing. That is, simply tell the adolescent what he/she has just said or done.

Examples

Situation 1: After you ask how he/she is doing, the adolescent tells you about a problem with a friend.

Content Summary: "So, you're having troubles with your friend."

Situation 2: A girl tells you about her weekend. She says that she went to a movie with a group of girls and afterwards had a fight with her boyfriend who didn't like her friends.

Content Summary: "Your boyfriend doesn't like your friends and it caused you to get into a fight."

Summarizing Feelings

Sometimes your Pilot will tell or show you some of his/her feelings. These emotions may be pleasant, unpleasant, or both. Whenever you notice an emotion in your Pilot, try to identify a word that seems to best describe that feeling. Then, add this feeling word to your summarization of content. Note that if you hear both pleasant and unpleasant emotions, you may need to include more than one feeling word in your statement.

Don't worry too much about sounding like an "echo chamber" when you tell your Pilot a summary of what he/she said. Adolescents enjoy it when someone repeats back the key points that they are saying. This shows them you care and are very interested in how they feel about things.

Examples

Situation 1: A boy smiles as he tells you about how he was shocked that he received an "A" on a very difficult test.

Feeling Summary: "You are amazed that you aced that test!"

Situation 2: A tall girl talks to you about how she keeps growing and "hates" that she is bigger than all of her friends.

Feeling Summary: "You are upset that you are so much taller than your friends."

Situation 3: A boy tells you that he visited a college and loved it. He would like to go there after high school, but he doesn't believe that his grades will be good enough to get in.

Feeling Summary: "You really liked that college, but you are worried that your grades will keep you from being accepted."

Hint: In addition to using your words, try to show with your face and voice that you understand and care about the feelings you sense your Pilot is experiencing.

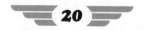

Activity 2.3:   Constructing Summaries

Directions: For each of the following statements from adolescents, write the best summary you can. Try to include one or more feeling words in each summary.

Katie: "My mom won't let me have anything but a stupid little turtle. She doesn't understand how much I've always wanted a puppy."

Phillip: "This grading period, I think I'm going to do much better than I did before. Already, I've got 'A's' and 'B's' in all my classes. . . except for one!"

Sabrina: "I hate this school and everyone in it! Man, I can't wait to get out of here!"

Todd: "Did you see the game yesterday? That team is the best! They might even take the Superbowl this year. I wish I was big enough to play on the football team here at school."

Follow-Up:

Similar to the procedures you used in Activity 2.2, have one person in your group tell a brief description of something that happened to him/her during the past year. When the story is finished, brainstorm different ways to summarize content and/or feelings. Be sure that each summarization does not add new information, or end with a question. Rather, a good summarization shows that you are listening carefully and encouraging the talker to continue sharing with you.

4. Use Strategic Self-Disclosures

Self-Disclosure can be a very effective way to communicate to your Pilot that you have some experiences similar to his/her situation. Sometimes, telling your story to your Pilot can be very effective in helping you show that you understand. But, if your story is dragged out or off the topic, it can also backfire and convince the adolescent that you are not very understanding. To be effective, self-disclosures must be brief, relevant, and timely.

As you get to know your adolescent better, it may be helpful to think of one or more stories you can share about yourself that may be similar to his/her experiences. Then, build a strategy of how to share your story briefly, while making it relevant to the young person. Next, determine the best time and place to tell it.

Activity 2.4: Building a Plan for Self-Disclosure

Directions: Pair up with another Co-Pilot and exchange handbooks. Take turns using the following questions to interview each other. Write summaries of your partner's responses in his/her book.

1. What is one of your interests or hobbies?

2. What is one of your greatest personal strengths or characteristics?

3. What is one challenge you had when you were a teenager?

4. What was one of your greatest accomplishments when you were a teenager?

Follow-Up:

Look over your responses that your partner wrote in your book. Discuss some good and bad times for sharing this information with an adolescent.

Chapter 3

Take Off and Landing Procedures

"If you fly high or far enough, you'll always find a place where the sun is shining."

Amelia Earhart*

*Amelia Earhart was the first female pilot to fly solo across the Atlantic Ocean. Amelia was lost at sea, presumably in a plane crash, while she was attempting to break another record by flying around the world.

Take Off and Landing Procedures

Like any mentoring relationship, Co-Piloting has three stages: a beginning stage (Take Off), a middle stage (In–Flight), and an ending stage (Landing). Each of these stages involves its own set of challenges and opportunities. Giving careful consideration to the dynamics of each stage will help ensure that you and your Co-Pilot will have a safe and successful journey. This Chapter will emphasize the first and third stages.

Take Off

In the beginning you will want to say and do things to help your relationship get off the ground with your Pilot. Your first meetings together will help you build a foundation that will help strengthen and sustain your relationship over time.

In–Flight

Once the relationship has taken off, you will need to keep the momentum going. For helpful suggestions to use in this phase, refer to Chapters 4 and 5 in this book. In addition, the activities in the "Self-Improvement Lessons" will provide opportunities to help you and your Pilot explore a variety of relevant topics together.

Landing

Preparing for your journey's end with your Pilot takes careful planning. If approached carefully, this transition in your relationship can be meaningful and memorable for both of you.

Take Off

Most adolescents are thrilled to have their own Co-Pilots. They are excited to have someone like you take such a special interest in them. In the beginning, like flying an airplane, you will want to follow certain procedures with your Pilot to help the relationship take off smoothly. To do this, feel free to use your own personal way of relating to young people your Pilot's age.

If your mentoring relationship doesn't take off immediately with your Pilot, don't take it personally. Several reasons could account for a slow take off. Some adolescents, for example, may not easily build trust toward someone like you. You might, for example, remind your Pilot of someone in his/her past who belittled, ignored, or abandoned him/her. Another possible reason may be the Pilot's shyness. Withdrawn adolescents, for example, may require extra Co-Pilot patience until they become more comfortable with the relationship. Other reasons a Pilot might be reluctant to bond with you are covered in Chapter 5.

Taking off in your relationship with a young person may require you to be very patient and determined. Hang in there! There are countless examples of adolescents who eventually came around in the relationship, due to their Co-Pilots' caring and persistence. On the next pages you will find several ideas that can help you achieve a smooth take off.

In the Beginning

1. Clarify Expectations:

Briefly introduce yourself and give a description of a Pilot and Co-Pilot. Check out your Pilot's understanding of and feelings toward the program. Also clarify where, when, and for how long you will be meeting together as Pilot and Co-Pilot.

2. Discuss Confidentiality:

Explain to your Pilot that you will keep private what he/she says, unless you are told about something that involves danger. Then you must tell your Program Coordinator about the situation so that you can be sure everyone will be safe.

Note that even if your Pilot shares with you information about past abuse or potential harm, you must tell your Program Coordinator. See page 37 for a sample statement you could use to explain this to your Pilot.

3. Encourage Your Pilot to Respond:

Be sure to ask your Pilot if he/she has any questions or feelings about the program. Give him/her another chance to share any curiosities or uncertainties he/she might have. Remember, if your Pilot is somewhat unresponsive, don't take it personally. Allow your relationship to develop over time.

4. Get to Know your Pilot and Have Some Fun:

In the beginning of any mentoring relationship, it is important to take things slow and easy. Be playful and have some fun times together. On the next pages, you will find lists of ice-breaking questions and activities to help your relationship take off. You may want to look through these lists again prior to your first meeting with your Pilot.

Activity 3.1: Ice-Breaking Questions

Directions: The following are sample questions you can ask your Pilot to help "break the ice" during your first few meetings. Practice using these questions with other Co-Pilots in your training group. When using these questions with your Pilot, share some of your own answers.

1. What is your favorite (least favorite) kind of music? TV show? Sport? School subject? Story? Animal? Place to go? Time of year?

2. What do you like to do when you are not in school?

3. If you had all the money you would need to go anywhere you wanted, where would you go?

4. What is a special interest (or hobby) that you have?

5. What are some things that you can do very well?

6. What is one thing that you wish you could learn to do better?

7. What do you hope to be doing five years from now? Ten years from now?

8. What do you look for in a friend?

9. When have you felt proud? Embarrassed? Afraid? Angry? Sad? Grateful?

10. If you could, what would you change about the world? School? Your friends? Yourself? Your situation?

11. When have you helped someone? What motivated you to reach out to that person?

12. Who is your hero/heroine? What do you like so much about the person?

13. What was a nightmare you once had?

14. You have been selected to go on a two month expedition to search for new life on Mars. You will already be taking everything you need to survive. You are allowed to choose three additional things to take with you. What will you take?

Other Ice Breakers

Here is a list of other activities that may help you and your Pilot take off in your relationship.

1. Play a sport such as basketball. Play catch with a baseball or football. If you are not skilled at these activities, but your Pilot likes them, let him/her teach you.

2. Play a favorite noncompetitive game. For example, noncompetitive board games are available in some amusement stores. Try to limit most of the games you play to those which are noncompetitive or cooperative in nature. You may want to check with your Pilot's school counselor to determine if he/she has a noncompetitive game you can borrow.

3. Have breakfast or lunch with your Pilot at school. This may be a one time or weekly event.

4. Meet with the other Pilots and Co-Pilots in your program for group ice-breaking activities. Hint: This could take place in the school gym, cafeteria, field, or at a local recreational facility.

5. Ask your Pilot to show you a talent or interest that he/she has such as drawing, painting, photography, playing a musical instrument, rapping, poetry, athletic skill, or performing a magic trick.

6. Ask your Pilot to share some of his/her achievements in or outside of school.

7. Develop a "special handshake" with your Pilot which you will use whenever you meet. This may be more appropriate for younger adolescent Pilots.

Landing

Sadly, every journey must come to an end. However, the ending of your Co-Piloting relationship should not be thought of as a "relationship termination." Rather, it is a "transition period." Both you and your Pilot may be sad and need to grieve in some way as your relationship nears this time. It is best if this grieving process begins well before the final meeting.

Landing can actually become a very "uplifting" experience, if approached carefully and systematically. Here is a list of suggestions that will help you and your Pilot derive the most benefit from this process.

1. **Prepare Early:** If possible, begin preparing your Pilot at least three weeks before your final meeting. Remind your Pilot periodically when your last meeting will take place.

2. **Review Highlights:** Recall some of the smooth and turbulent times during your relationship.

3. **Share Feelings Openly:** Encourage discussions about concluding your time together.

4. **Reaffirm Strengths in Each Other:** Talk about the positive qualities you found in each other during your relationship.

5. **Avoid New Issues:** Ensure that your final meeting time does not include the discussion of new issues that will need to be resolved. If your Pilot brings up a new concern, either refer him/her to your Program Coordinator, or deal with the situation and postpone your final meeting to another time. Then try once again to "avoid new issues."

6. **Exchange Written Words:** Share with one another good-bye letters or cards. You may want to write or type a letter for your pilot that can be included in his/her "Pilot Portfolio" (See page 50).

7. **End on a "High:"** Be sure to laugh and have some fun during your last formal meeting together. Remember, "When saying good-bye. . . end on a high!"

Activity 3.2: Safe Landing
(A Simulation)

Directions: This activity is a simulation of what it can be like to help your Pilot have a safe landing in your relationship. It works best if you have at least eight participants. If you don't have eight Co-Pilots to participate, merely read through this activity. Then discuss with your group answers to the questions in the "Follow-Up" section.

You will need some room to move around. One volunteer will become a "pilot" who will pretend to make a difficult landing on a runway. Another volunteer will become the "air-traffic controller" who is in the airport control tower attempting to help the "pilot" land safely.

All the other participants should stand in two, equally long parallel lines, with each person in one line facing towards people in the other line. This is the "airport landing strip." The "pilot" should stand between the lines at one end, and the "air-traffic controller" should stand at the opposite end in the "control tower."

Here is the story: The "pilot" is flying solo and coming in for a difficult landing. (Place a blindfold, or equivalent, over the eyes of the "pilot" to represent poor visibility). The "air-traffic controller" must talk the "pilot" down for a safe landing. The "air-traffic controller" and "pilot" can talk back-and-forth with one another (by radio). Using dialog only, the "pilot" must be guided from one side of the runway to the other, where the "co-pilot" is standing. When the "pilot" finally reaches the "air-traffic controller" a safe landing has occurred and the activity is finished.

Hints: After blindfolding the "pilot" turn him/her around about three times. Then, several people should place objects or themselves on the runway to represent debris from a storm. People nearby should ensure the "pilot" doesn't fall as he/she approaches the more difficult obstacles.

Follow-Up:

1. What was it like for the "pilot" when he/she discovered that a blindfold would be worn and that later, obstacles would be placed on the runway? How might this experience be similar to the time when your Pilot approaches the final landing of your relationship?

2. In this simulation, what were the "air traffic controller's" responsibilities? How are these similar to your responsibilities in landing your relationship with your Pilot?

3. How well did the "air-traffic controller" in this simulation reassure the "pilot?" How can you reassure your Pilot during your landing?

4. How well did the "air-traffic controller" in this simulation invite the "pilot" to communicate his/her thoughts and feelings? How can you invite your Pilot to share as you approach the landing of your relationship?

Chapter 4

Handling Turbulence

"When the going gets tough, just about all you can do is keep going forward, and press on."

Chuck Yeager*

* Chuck Yeager was a professional test pilot. Among his many accomplishments was his record breaking flight in which he was the first human being to travel faster than the speed of sound.

Handling Turbulence

Though Co-Piloting can be a very enjoyable and fulfilling experience for you and your Pilot, there may be some "turbulence" ahead. However, these challenging times can be turned into powerful opportunities to break new ground with your Pilot. Many Co-Pilots and Pilots have said that getting through a difficult time together was one of the most helpful experiences they had in the program.

When real pilots are faced with a stormy weather situation, they (along with their crew and control tower personnel) must consider the severity of the situation and their own limitations before deciding how they will proceed. In some cases, the best method to handle turbulence is to fly over or around the storm. Other times, a decision is made to patiently wait for a better time to take off. Sometimes, the pilot may fly directly into the storm knowing that he/or she has the skills and support to handle the situation.

Similarly, you and your Pilot may encounter some turbulent times during your work together. When you do, you will need to consider your own limitations and have several courses of action from which to choose.

Knowing Your Limitations

You should become clearly aware of your limitations as a Co-Pilot so that you can set boundaries in your relationship with your Pilot. Unfortunately, some difficult situations may arise in which it is not clear how you should proceed. The following descriptions of Co-Pilot limitations can help you know what to do in most situations. If, after considering these limitations, you continue to feel unsure about how to proceed, you should seek guidance from your Program Coordinator, fellow Co-Pilots, or other resource people who are available to you.

1. Training: If your Pilot ever requires assistance that is beyond your skill level, you will need to know how to make appropriate referrals (see "Making Referrals" on pages 46 and 47). If you encounter such a situation, ask your Program Coordinator for guidance. For example, if you have not had specific training in addictions and family systems, you should not give advice to your Pilot on how to handle an alcoholic parent. By giving untrained advice in such cases, caring people have sometimes unknowingly contributed to the family's problems. Instead, you may want to accompany your Pilot to a first session with a counselor, social worker, or other professional who is trained in this area.

2. Confidentiality: Another critical limitation is that you may not always be able to keep everything your Pilot tells you secret. When your Pilot informs you about past, present, or potential harm to him/herself or others, it must be reported. If your Pilot tells you, for example, about being abused, you cannot keep this a secret. You must inform your Program Coordinator or other person to whom you've been directed to give this information.

One way to tell an adolescent about your limits to confidentiality is to make a statement like the following:

Anything you say in here is just between you and me. But, if you ever tell me about something dangerous to you or someone else, then I will have to tell (give the name of the Program Coordinator) about it. This is because I care about you and have to make sure you and others are safe.

3. Time: You may find that your Pilot occasionally may not want to stop your meeting when you need to leave. In this situation, it is important to take care of your needs by setting clear boundaries for your time together. Do not let your Pilot extend your meeting time through manipulation. It may help to let your Pilot know when only five minutes remain in the session. This will provide your teen with a final opportunity to cover anything else he/she would like to talk about.

4. Energy: Sometimes, your personal energy may be at a lower level than usual. When this occurs, don't force yourself to "hang in there" while trying to hide yawns. Be honest with your Pilot. Perhaps taking a walk together or moving to another location will help. If this doesn't work, end the meeting with an invitation to make up the time on another day. Ending the session like this may be disappointing to your Pilot, but your honesty can provide a valuable lesson.

5. Issue Sensitivity: Most of us have certain issues that seem to really bother us. We each have our own set of pet peeves. Be sure that your sensitivities don't interfere in your relationship with your Pilot. If you ever believe you are becoming oversensitive about some things your Pilot says or does, share this with your Co-Pilot Support Group or Program Coordinator. They can help you brainstorm some other approaches to the situation.

If your Pilot says or does something that alarms you, be careful not to overreact. Be a good listener and share your concerns about the issue with your Co-Pilot Support Group or Program Supervisor.

6. Closeness: You and your Pilot may develop close feelings toward one another. This is expected and encouraged up to a point. Be cautious with physical touch, but do not avoid an opportunity to shake hands with your Pilot. For example, developing a "secret handshake" is probably going to be okay.

In addition, we do not recommend that you take your Pilot alone to your home. Although many Co-Pilots have taken their Pilots to sporting events, shows, and shopping malls, it is safer to do this in a group. If you and your Pilot plan to meet outside of the regularly planned Co-Pilot program, check with your Program Coordinator and be sure to acquire parental/guardian permission.

Activity 4.1: Co-Pilot Limitations

Directions: Gather in a small group with other Co-Pilots. Together, develop a humorous skit in which one of you (Co-Pilot) is faced with a situation which raises one of the six Co-Pilot limitation issues just described. Be sure to involve each of your group members in the skit. Develop a clear beginning to your skit but leave the ending open, with the Co-Pilot unsure how to proceed.

Act out your skit in front of the other Co-Pilots. When finished, invite the audience to brainstorm and evaluate different approaches the Co-Pilot might have used in the situation.

Pilot Resistance

As mentioned earlier, your Pilot at some time may become resistant in your relationship. This resistance may only occur during a few meetings, or it may last for a few months. If you observe this in your Pilot, be sure not to take it personally. Remember, you will be working with a young person who has probably never met anyone quite like you. It may take some time for you to become comfortable with each other.

Behavioral Indicators of Resistance

The following behaviors, if they are frequently and continually observed, may indicate that your Pilot is resisting the relationship. If these behaviors continue for more than two meetings, seek guidance from your Program Coordinator and/or Co-Pilot Support Group.

☐ Absent from your meetings
☐ Quiet and not talkative
☐ Uncooperative
☐ Oppositional body language
  (such as rolling his/her eyes)

Reasons Behind Pilot Resistance

If you believe your Pilot is being resistant, consider the following possible reasons:

▷ **Mandatory or "Pushed" Involvement:** The adolescent may resent the fact that he/she did not have a choice in the matter.

▷ **Unfamiliar Territory:** The adolescent sees the Co-Pilot as someone who is quite different from him/her and is unsure how to relate. There may also be a fear of intimacy, fear of closeness and fear of loss.

▷ **Fear of Loss:** The adolescent is afraid to allow any relationship to develop that might result in emotional pain.

▷ **Peer Influence:** The adolescent is afraid that his/her peers will ridicule him/her for having a mentor.

40

Activity 4.2: Handling Resistance

Directions: Look through the five ways to handle Pilot resistance described on the next page. Break up into triads (groups of three) and give each group a few minutes to develop a humorous skit showing resistance. Within each triad, label one person as the "Pilot," another as the "Co-Pilot," and the third as the "Observer." Have the Pilot play the role of a mildly resistant adolescent. He/she might begin by acting bored and frustrated with the Co-Pilot's efforts to hold a conversation about schoolwork.

Before the skit reaches its conclusion, the participants should stop and brainstorm some possible ways to approach the Pilot. The five "Tips" listed on the next page may be helpful to consider. Then, resume the skit, trying out one or more of the ideas that were discussed. Note that the person acting as the Pilot should allow the strategies to be successful.

Finally, hold a group discussion about the skit and about each of the "Tips for Handling Resistance." Brainstorm examples of when these tips might be useful with Pilots in different situations.

Tips for Handling Resistance

1. **Do More and Talk Less.** Back off from asking too many questions and invite your Pilot to do some activities with you. For example, take a walk, play catch, or play a game. Chapter 4 will provide you with several other involving activities which you can do with your Pilot.

2. **Follow the Pilot's Lead.** As much as possible, let your Pilot determine what you will be doing or talking about during your time together. Use more of a learner/follower approach rather than a leader/teacher approach, especially in the beginning of the relationship. Later, after the relationship builds, your Pilot will be more receptive to your taking the lead sometimes.

3. **Be Persistent.** Don't give up. Some Co-Pilots who became discouraged and thought of quitting the relationship, discovered that their sheer determination finally paid off. Persistence is one way you can show your Pilot you are more genuinely caring than other "helpers" he/she has known.

4. **Try Yielding.** If working with your Pilot feels like trying to open a locked door, try "yielding." This is a term used in some martial art styles that describes a creative backing-off approach as a way to weaken an opponent's attack. You can try this backing-off from your Pilot's resisting behaviors by acknowledging your feelings of discouragement. Invite your Pilot to reveal his/her real feelings about working with you. If your Pilot discloses any feelings to you, listen to them carefully. This strategy may provide the "break through" opportunity for which you have been hoping. It can provide a new beginning in your relationship.

5. **Seek Assistance.** If all else fails, explore the situation with your Program Coordinator and/or Co-Pilot Support Group.

Tips for Handling Other Challenges

When your Pilot:

☐ **Is easily distracted during your conversations.**
Tip: Check with the Pilot's counselor, teachers, and/or parents to find out if this is typical behavior for the adolescent. Provide feedback to your Pilot about this behavior. Then, ask what might be the reasons behind the behavior. Explore together what each of you might do differently to help improve the situation.

☐ **Resists ending your meetings.**
Tip: Together, work out some way to cue the teen that there are five minutes remaining in your meeting. This could be done by using a hand signal or by telling him/her directly that the meeting is almost over. If the resistance continues, inform your Program Coordinator and/or your Co-Pilot Support Group.

☐ **Seems unappreciative of your efforts.**
Tip: Pilots should not be expected to express much appreciation for anything you do with them. Most teenagers eventually come to deeply value their mentors. But, some young people do not feel comfortable with, or know how to express these feelings.

☐ **Expresses intense emotions.**
Tip: Some adolescents and adults are uncomfortable when someone shows emotions. When your Pilot tells or shows you about his/her feelings, always become focused and be a good listener. It is important to show caring, accepting, and a desire to understand the teen's views. Try to avoid reassuring statements like "It's going to be okay" or"Tomorrow, you'll feel better about things." These statements are often interpreted as discounting their feelings about the situation. Also, avoid giving quick advice. Most young people, when they express intense emotions, don't want to be told what they should do. What they want most is someone who is a caring, patient listener.

☐ Procrastinates.

Tip: All of us put things off sometimes. However, if this is a frequent behavior for your Pilot, it is probably causing problems for him/her. Ask your Pilot to work through the Self-Improvement Lessons later in this book, in particular Lessons 1 and 4. Then help your Pilot set some short term goals that he/she can accomplish within a set amount of time. Provide an incentive to help motivate your Pilot. For example, allow your Pilot to earn extra time to participate in a special activity with you.

☐ Has low self-esteem.

Tip: Self-esteem consists of two parts, self-confidence (how capable we believe we are) and self-worth (how valuable we believe we are). To help raise your Pilot's self-confidence, you might start by focusing on Self-Improvement Lessons 1, 2, 3, and 14 in this book. But raising your Pilot's self-confidence may take more than a set of activities. It may require you and others to provide a lot of encouragement and recognition over a long period of time.

To help raise self-worth, you will need to help your Pilot view him/herself as valuable and worthwhile. By simply giving your valuable time and energy, you will show your Pilot that at least someone believes that he/she has value. In addition, you will help build up your Pilot through consistent affirmations or compliments about his/her personal strengths (see in particular Self-Improvement Lesson 1).

☐ Seems to be holding a lot of anger inside.

Tip: Share with your Pilot your observations that led you to this impression. Then, encourage him/her to share the underlying reasons. It may help your Pilot to go through Self-Improvement Lessons 12 and 14. If your Pilot continues to express angry feelings, see your Program Coordinator for some other ideas.

☐ Gets into trouble with misbehavior at school.

Tip: Don't focus most of your time together on your Pilot's behavior difficulties. Depending on your Pilot's age and abilities, help him/her first set a goal on which to work. Then brainstorm alternative approaches your Pilot could use to reach that goal. Next, encourage your Pilot to practice these different approaches by role-playing with you. You might begin by working through Self-Improvement Lessons 3, 8, 12, ad 13.

☐ Has parents or guardians who are not cooperative with your efforts.

Tip: It is important to build a positive relationship with your Pilot's parents or guardians. Some Co-Pilots visit their Pilots' homes at the beginning of the relationship while other Co-Pilots make regular home visits. Allow the parents or guardians to get to know you and encourage them to share their perspectives. Help them feel involved in your work by asking for suggestions for working with their child.

Making Referrals

When to Refer Your Pilot

There are several situations in which you should refer your Pilot immediately to the appropriate professional helper. For example, think about your potential referral sources if you discovered that your Pilot was:

☐ Acting out sexually.

☐ Involved in illegal activities with a group of older adolescents.

☐ Considering running away from home.

☐ Being threatened by older youths.

☐ Threatening to harm him/herself or someone else.

☐ Experiencing prolonged or intense fear, anger, or depression.

☐ Raising questions that you believe someone else could answer better than you.

☐ Bragging about finding a weapon.

How to Refer Your Pilot

When making a referral, you may find the following suggestions helpful:

1. Listen to your Pilot's feelings in a caring and open manner.

2. Express your personal support for your Pilot and your concern about the situation.

3. Remind your Pilot of your limited training in dealing with this kind of situation.

4. Offer to go with your Pilot and tell about the situation to a professional helper.

5. Follow-up with your Pilot and/or referral person to ensure that assistance is being provided.

6. Continue meeting with your Pilot, listening and providing encouragement.

Activity 4.3: List of Referral Resources

Directions: Know the best person to whom you will refer your Pilot for different situations. Complete the following list of resources so you will have it at your fingertips if you ever need it.

Co-Pilot Coordinator:
_____

How to Contact:
_____
_____

Pilot's Information:
Name:
_____
Address:
_____
_____
Phone:_____

Home Contact(s):
_____
_____

How to Contact:
_____
_____

Other Family Contact(s):
_____
_____
_____
_____
_____

School Information:
Address:
_____
_____
Phone: _____
Teachers:
_____
_____
Counselor:
_____
Phone: _____
Other School Contact:
_____

Community Resources:
_____
_____
_____
_____
_____
_____

Other:
_____
_____
_____
_____

Chapter 5

Projects for You and Your Pilot

"Tell me and I'll forget.
Show me, and I may not remember.
Involve me, and I'll understand."

Native American saying

Projects for You and Your Pilot

Once you begin meeting with your Pilot, you may want to spend a lot of your time talking together. However, some caution is important here. Be careful not to give your Pilot the impression that you are trying to be his/her counselor or psychologist. Too much talking may eventually result in your Pilot pulling away emotionally from you.

Ensure that you and your Pilot become involved together in some fun, meaningful activities or projects. This chapter will provide a collection of games and activities that will help you and your Pilot have fun and memorable experiences together.

Pilot Portfolio

Use the following list to help your Pilot develop a portfolio about him/herself. You will need to acquire some kind of device for holding pages, such as a folder with pockets or a three-ring notebook with inserts. You might provide some construction paper and other art supplies which you and your Pilot can use to make the portfolio. Compiling this material is best accomplished as an ongoing activity with the periodic adding of materials.

Portfolio Contents

1. Introduction (A brief description with a photograph, if possible)
2. List of Personal Interests and Preferences (See Activity 3.1)
3. Favorite Activities
4. Strengths (See Chapter 6, Lesson 1)
5. Personal Goals
6. Successes and Accomplishments
7. Complimentary Letters About the Pilot
8. Sample Work
    - Schoolwork
    - Artwork
    - Poems
    - Song/Rap Lyrics
    - Stories
    - Photographs
    - Other Projects

60 Games and Activities for Pilots/Co-Pilots

Games

- ☐ Play non-competitive board games.
- ☐ Play computer games designed for two people.
- ☐ Do a scavenger hunt together.
- ☐ Make up a game together and play it.

Creative Arts

- ☐ Make a "Me Collage" (a collection of pictures/words that describe your Pilot).
- ☐ Design a personal coat-of-arms (with symbols that describe your Pilot).
- ☐ Make an "I Can" (a can covered with cut-out pictures of eyes from magazines) and fill it with statements about what your Pilot can do well.
- ☐ Write and/or sing a rap song about Co-Piloting.
- ☐ Make up a skit on a certain topic and present it to the class.
- ☐ Have your Pilot play his/her favorite music and discuss its meaning.
- ☐ Design and create a presentation for a school bulletin board.
- ☐ Create a display for a multicultural fair.

Sports/Athletics

- ☐ Shoot baskets (basketball).
- ☐ Play catch (baseball, football).
- ☐ Have the Pilot show or teach you about a sport or athletic skill.
- ☐ Exercise together (jog, walk, aerobics, etc.).
- ☐ Collect information about athletes and/or teams.
- ☐ Attend a sporting event together.
- ☐ Arrange for your Pilot to meet a college or professional athlete.

Service Learning

☐ Create a "care package" or other gift for a needy student or family.

☐ Volunteer together to be "Meeters and Greeters" at one or more Parent Teacher Organization meetings.

☐ Give time to a local animal welfare society.

☐ Volunteer together to provide "foster" care for an abandoned animal until a permanent home can be found for it.

☐ Adopt a place on the school grounds to keep clean.

☐ Manage a booth at a school fair or carnival.

☐ Plant a tree, bush, or flower.

☐ Adopt a nursing home resident and visit him/her weekly.

☐ Make a presentation to younger students about a topic such as tobacco or alcohol/drugs. Be sure the lesson is age-appropriate.

☐ Assist a teacher in the classroom.

☐ Construct something that a teacher can use in the classroom.

☐ Volunteer together for a fundraising activity.

☐ Assist with the school store.

☐ Help decorate the school or other community building for a holiday.

Academic Encouragement

☐ Take turns reading to a child.

☐ Write a story together using mostly the Pilot's ideas.

☐ Study together (homework and test preparation).

☐ Take turns reading to each other (stories, newspaper/magazine articles, homework, reading assignments).

☐ Make a presentation together to a younger group of students about "How to Study Better."

☐ Develop a schedule chart for study times.

☐ Work together to clean out and organize Pilot's notebook(s), book bag, and/or locker (with your Pilot's permission).

☐ Work on other study skills.

☐ Visit the school media center or public library together.

Career Exploration

☐ Help out on "Career Day."

☐ Build a special project together and put it on display.

☐ Volunteer at school functions.

☐ Arrange for your Pilot to take a career interest test and talk about the results.

☐ Visit and interview people in various careers.

☐ Arrange for your Pilot to "shadow" you at your job site.

☐ Visit the vocational program at a nearby high school.

☐ Check out different kinds of careers in the school library or career center.

Other Activities

☐ Have your Pilot keep a "Success Journal" (a diary of daily accomplishments).

☐ Cook a special meal together.

☐ Sew something together.

☐ Plan an outing or activity with the other Pilots and Co-Pilots.

☐ Take a walk around the school grounds or park just to talk.

☐ Participate in a ropes course with other Pilots and Co-Pilots.

☐ Have breakfast or lunch together at the school.

☐ Have a meal together at a restaurant.

☐ Learn to perform a magic trick together.

☐ Challenge each other to reach some personal goal.

Chapter 6

Self-Improvement Lessons for Pilots

"The future of [humankind] lies waiting for those who will come to understand their lives and take up their responsibilities to all living things."

Vine Victor Deloria, Jr.*

*Vine Victor Deloria, Jr. is an author and Native American rights leader.

Self-Improvement
Lessons for Pilots

On the following pages, you will find fifteen lessons each containing information and activities that can be used as discussion starters with your Pilot. Each can help you discuss with your Pilot important issues in his/her life and explore various strategies for dealing with them.

Recommendations:

1. If your Pilot has the ability, encourage him/her to read some of these lessons with you. Occasionally stop and make sure your Pilot is understanding what you are reading. Once you have read a story or activity, discuss the information.

2. The 15 lessons contain quotes, stories, checklists, and activities that provide opportunities for you and your Pilot to have discussions on a variety of important issues. Be open and honest with your views while being a good listener as your Pilot expresses his/her opinions.

3. Use these lessons occasionally, not during every meeting. Remember that the lessons should not become the primary work you do with your Pilot. They are intended to help you both focus on some important aspects of personal development. Use the quotes, stories, and activities to help you start discussions with your Pilot. Then, encourage your Pilot to explore how the information relates to him/her.

4. Don't worry too much about the sequence in which you cover these lessons with your Pilot. You and/or your Pilot may select lessons that seem most interesting or relevant. Also, don't push to complete every part of each lesson in sequence. Let your Pilot help decide what to cover.

5. Feel free to slow down and take extra time with some stories or activities. You might find that something you are covering provides a timely learning opportunity for your Pilot.

6. Your Pilot may want to include some of the products of these activities in his/her Pilot Portfolio.

THE FIFTEEN LESSONS

1. **Personal Strengths**
2. **Character Building**
3. **Goal Setting**
4. **Study Habits and Skills**
5. **Career Exploration**
6. **Family**
7. **Healthy Relationships**
8. **Peer Pressure**
9. **Stress**
10. **Alcohol**
11. **Other Drugs**
12. **Anger Management**
13. **Conflict Resolution**
14. **Being Assertive**
15. **Racism**

LESSON 1: PERSONAL STRENGTHS

"Learning about one's personal strengths is an important step toward building the kind of self-confidence and positive motivation that can last a lifetime."

Anonymous

What do you think of when you hear "personal strength?" Many adolescents think of how physically strong they are or how well they can perform in an athletic event or sport. Others may think about how well they are doing in particular subjects in school. However, a person has many more strengths than just athletic and academic abilities.

Mary's Story

Mary was a seventeen year old who was in a special class for adolescents with low IQ scores. She was small for her age and not very athletic. One spring, she was traveling in a small airplane to visit her father who lived in a village in Alaska. An unexpectedly fierce blizzard caused the plane to make a crash landing in the mountains, far from civilization. Both pilots suffered broken legs and the only other passenger besides Mary was knocked unconscious. Fortunately Mary was only slightly hurt.

For the next few days, Mary gathered edible plants and rigged a device that would gather the sun's heat to melt snow for water. She also ripped apart the plane seat and used the material and stuffing to help keep the injured people warm.

Mary was able to keep all three of them alive for more than a week until they were finally discovered by a rescue party. Through Mary's persistence, caring, knowledge of survival strategies, and will to survive, she saved her own life as well as the lives of the others.

Most people in Mary's neighborhood were not aware that she had many strengths. She had never excelled in a sport or in her schoolwork as compared to others her age. However, Mary had several strengths others her age did not have. They included knowledge, skills, and abilities which she used to help herself and her companions survive a life-threatening experience.

Discussion Questions:

1. How do you think Mary gained her personal strengths?

2. Do you believe the following quote? Why or why not? "Everyone is a genius in some way."

3. How can it help someone to learn about his/her personal strengths?

Personal Strength Words

1. Look through the list of "90 Personal Strength Words" on the next page. Place a "P" in front of the words that best describe your personal strengths. Place a "C" in front of any that describe your Co-Pilot's strengths.

2. Discuss how your list of words differs from your Co-Pilot's list. How are they similar?

3. Explore how each of you have used your personal strengths to:
   • Survive an emergency situation.
   • Cope with someone who is not friendly with you.
   • Start working toward a goal that you have been putting off.
   • Finish a project that you are tired of.
   • Bring about a success in school.
   • Bring about a success outside of school.

90 Personal Strength Words

A
___Accepting
___Adventurous
___Appreciative
___Artistic
___Assertive
___Athletic

B
___Bold
___Brave
___Bright

C
___Calm
___Caring
___Cautious
___Clever
___Confident
___Considerate
___Cooperative
___Courageous
___Courteous
___Creative
___Curious

D
___Dedicated
___Dependable
___Determined
___Devoted
___Disciplined

E
___Eager
___Efficient
___Encouraging
___Energetic
___Enthusiastic

F
___Fair
___Faithful

___Flexible
___Forgiving
___Friendly
___Fun-Loving

G
___Generous
___Gentle
___Giving
___Good Sport

H
___Hard Worker
___Helpful
___Honest
___Humble
___Humorous

I
___Independent
___Insightful
___Interested
___Involved

L
___Laidback
___Leader
___Likable
___Loving
___Loyal

M
___Mature
___Motivated

N
___Neat
___Nurturing

O
___On Task
___Open–minded

___Optimistic
___Organized

P
___Patient
___Perceptive
___Persevering
___Positive
___Prepared
___Punctual

Q
___Quiet

R
___Reasonable
___Reliable
___Resourceful
___Respectful

S
___Self-Aware
___Sensitive
___Sharing
___Sincere
___Supportive
___Survivalist

T
___Team Player
___Thoughtful
___Tolerant
___Trustworthy

U
___Understanding
___Unique
___Unselfish

W
___Warm
___Witty

Optional Activities

1. Have you and your Co-Pilot make lists of your five most important personal strengths. Take turns telling about when you've used the strengths on your list.

2. Find an object that symbolizes your list of "Personal Strength Words." If the object is small enough, carry it around with you as a reminder of your personal strengths.

3. Think of other people you both have known or heard about, that show some of your same personal strengths.

LESSON 2: CHARACTER BUILDING

"Character is like a tree and reputation like its shadow. The shadow is what we think of it; the tree is the real thing."
Abraham Lincoln

Being successful means more than merely having money, power, and other things that show your accomplishments. These things are merely signs that you have achieved something. They do not show what kind of person you are on the inside. Character building is one way to work on your inner self. It focuses on working to improve your beliefs and attitudes about yourself and others.

Charles Lindbergh's Story *

Charles Lindbergh was one of the most famous heroes of the 20th century. He was the first pilot to fly an airplane nonstop across the Atlantic Ocean between the United States and Europe. Lindbergh was a shy, quiet young man when he accomplished this feat. Many people remember him only for this heroic flight. But, Lindbergh was also someone who had many personal difficulties in his life. For example, he and his wife had a baby who was kidnapped and murdered.

In spite of his personal successes and problems, Lindbergh worked throughout his life on his own personal character. That is, he thought about his personality and his beliefs about things and kept working to improve himself. The following is his own description of his character building technique.

Lindbergh's Character Technique *

At night I would read off my list of character factors, and those which I had fulfilled satisfactorily during the day I would mark with a red (X); those I had not been called upon to demonstrate that day would get no mark. But those character factors which I had actually violated each day I would mark with a black (X). I began to check myself from day to day and compare my (marks) from month to month and year to year. I was glad to notice that there was an improvement as I grew older.

Charles Lindbergh

Discussion Questions:

1. How do you think people develop character? Where does it come from?

2. What are some kinds of situations that can affect our character for the better? For worse?

3. What kinds of character do you think helped Charles Lindbergh accomplish his famous flight? (Look through the following "Six Pillars of Character" for ideas.)

---

* From Mosley, (1976), p. 51.

The Six Pillars of Character

Trustworthiness

Respect

Responsibility

Justice & Fairness

Caring

Civic Virtue & Citizenship

Applying the "Six Pillars" to Our Lives

Under each of the following Six Pillars, you will find "Do's" and "Don'ts" that show us how we can apply each of these character traits to our lives. Take one Pillar at a time and explore each example under it. Both you and your Co-Pilot should try to think of a time when you or someone you know about showed this aspect of the Pillar. Perhaps you can complete a discussion of one Pillar during each of your meetings together.

Showing Character

I. TRUSTWORTHINESS
Worthy of trust, honor, and confidence

Honesty
Do's
☞ Tell the truth, the whole truth, and nothing but the truth.

☞ Be forthright, candid, and frank.

☞ Be sincere—say what you mean, mean what you say.

☞ If you find property, try to return it to its owner.

Don'ts
🛑 Don't betray a trust; strive to meet the legitimate expectations of those who trust you.

🛑 Don't lie (purposely misrepresenting facts or opinions).

🛑 Don't deliberately deceive or mislead by any means (concealing, distorting, telling half-truths).

🛑 Don't be devious or tricky.

🛑 Don't withhold important information in relationships of trust.

🛑 Don't steal another's property.

🛑 Don't cheat, defraud, or engage in tricks or deceptions.

Integrity and Courage
Do's
☞ Stand–up for your beliefs about right and wrong. Be yourself and resist social pressure to do things you think are wrong.

☞ "Walk your talk;" show commitment, courage, and self-discipline by doing the right thing regardless of personal cost.

Pages 69-73 reprinted from *Ethics: Easier Said Than Done*, with permission of the Josephson Institute of Ethics (c) 1992.

Promise-Keeping

Do's

☞ Be reliable, keep your word—pay your debts, return what you borrow.

☞ Make only those commitments that you firmly intend to keep and reasonably think you can keep.

Don'ts

🛑 Don't use tricky, unreasonable, or bad faith interpretations of the language of an agreement to evade commitments.

Fidelity and Loyalty

Do's

☞ Keep confidential information confidential; be discreet with private information that could be embarrassing or harmful to others.

☞ Within the limits of your other ethical obligations, be loyal by standing by, supporting, helping, and protecting your family, friends, teachers, employers, school, community, and country.

Don'ts

🛑 Don't talk behind people's backs, spread rumors, or engage in harmful gossip.

🛑 Don't violate other ethical principles in the name of loyalty—lying, cheating, stealing, or harming others to keep or win a friendship or gain approval.

🛑 Don't betray your loyalty by asking a friend to do something wrong to keep your friendship.

II. RESPECT

Regard for the dignity, worth, and autonomy of all persons (including self)

Do's

☞ Treat all people with respect by being courteous and polite.

☞ Respect the autonomy of others. Taking into account their age and maturity, respect the rights of individuals to make decisions about their own lives.

☞ Be tolerant, appreciative, and accepting of individual differences.

☞ Judge all people on their merits, not on their race, religion, nationality, gender, physical or mental condition, social or economic status, or any other improper factor.

Don'ts

🛑 Don't insult, abuse, demean, mistreat, or harass others.

🛑 Don't make inappropriate or unwanted comments about a person's race, religion, gender, or sexual orientation.

🛑 Don't use, manipulate, exploit, or take advantage of other people.

III. RESPONSIBILITY

Acknowledgement and performance of duties to others and self

Accountability

Do's

☞ Think before you act—consider the possible consequences on yourself and others and decide whether the act is honest, fair, caring, and respectful to all who will be affected.

☞ Be accountable; accept responsibility for the consequences of your actions and inactions.

☞ Be reliable; perform your duties.

☞ Set a good example with your own conduct; act as if someone whose respect you want is always watching.

☞ Take the initiative to make your society, school, or home life better for yourself and others.

Don'ts

🛑 Don't blame others for your mistakes or take credit for the achievements of others.

Pursuit of Excellence

Do's

☞ Do your best; make everything you do worthy of your pride.

☞ Be perseverant; meet your responsibilities even when it is difficult to do.

IV. JUSTICE & FAIRNESS

Making decisions that are just and fair.

Do's

☞ Treat all people fairly.

☞ Be open-minded, listen to others, and try to understand what they are saying and feeling.

☞ In making decisions, fairly consider all relevant information, including opposing viewpoints.

☞ Make decisions with impartiality based on consistent and appropriate standards.

Don'ts

🛑 Don't take unfair advantage of the mistakes or ignorance of others.

🛑 Don't take more than your fair share.

🛑 Don't let personal feelings interfere with decisions that should be made objectively.

V. CARING
Regard for the well-being of others

Do's

☞ Show that you care about others through kindness, caring, generosity, sharing, and compassion.

☞ Live by the Golden Rule—treat others the way you want them to treat you.

Don'ts

🛑 Don't be selfish, mean, cruel, or insensitive to the feelings of others.

VI. CIVIC VIRTUE & CITIZENSHIP
Recognition of and living up to social obligations

Do's

☞ Obey laws and school rules.

☞ Do your share; stay informed; vote; protect your family and community; and report crimes.

☞ Be charitable and altruistic.

Optional Activity

Use the Lindbergh method of character building. Make several photocopies of the "Six Pillars of Character" (see pages 67-73) and punch holes in them so they can be clipped in a three ring binder. Each day (or week), use one color pen (or marker) to check off which items you fulfilled. Use a different color to indicate those which you violated or make two lists each day, one of any character traits you fulfilled, the other of any traits you violated. Periodically, look back to see if you have made an improvement over time.

LESSON 3: GOAL SETTING

*"Dreams are airplanes that are in the sky.
Goals are the engines that
can make them fly."*

R. P. Bowman

Unfortunately, many young people don't think very often about setting positive and realistic goals for themselves. The most successful people know how to set an achievable, positive goal and then take action that will bring about goal attainment.

It has been said that "If you don't know where you are going, you will never get there." Unless you know how to make achievable plans for yourself, you will not find much success in your life.

Carl Lewis' Story *

Carl Lewis has set several world records and won numerous Olympic gold medals in track and field events. These remarkable achievements did not come easy for him. Growing up, Carl felt like the runt of the family and did not seem to have an aptitude for any sport. When young people in his neighborhood established teams for different sports, Carl was often the last one picked.

Despite his small size, Carl did not stop pursuing his dream of becoming a winning athlete. He wanted to find something he could do better than his sister. So he worked hard practicing for track events. He set his sights on one competition at a time and finally won the long jump competition in a regional Jesse Owens meet. Later, he continued to achieve one success after another until he became one of the most famous athletes in the world. Carl Lewis started with a dream, then worked hard to achieve one goal at a time until he finally reached and surpassed it.

For example, Carl used this technique of setting and achieving small goals when attempting a long jump. Just before a jump, he carefully planned each of his steps as a separate goal. Then he pictured in his mind his ultimate leap into the air. The results speak for themselves. In 1981, Carl broke the indoor long jump world record. In 1983, he became the first athlete in nearly a century to win three events in the national championships. In 1984, he won four gold medals in the Olympics and was named "Male Athlete of the Year" by the Associated Press two years in a row. Since then, Carl Lewis has won even more world championship events. In 1996, he was the second athlete to ever win gold medals in the same event (the long jump) in four Olympics.

Discussion Questions:
1. What is the importance of having a positive dream for your future? What are some of your dreams for your future?

2. What do you think are the main reasons people do not achieve their goals?

3. What can you learn from Carl Lewis' story that might help you?

* Adapted from Klots (1995) except for information about his 1996 Olympic achievement.

Long– and Short–Term Goals

You may have a dream that seems impossible for you to ever reach. Instead of becoming discouraged, try to focus on what your first step might be. Next, try to accomplish that first step to the best of your abilities. Then, plan other steps you will need to take and accomplish them one at a time. Each of these steps is called a short-term goal. Remember, a mountain can only be climbed one step at a time.

Long-Term Goals

Your dream is an accomplishment called a long-term goal. It may take you a long time before you finally reach it. What is a goal that you would like to accomplish:

- Within the next year? _____

- Within the next ten years? _____

- Within your lifetime? _____

Short-Term Goals

Once you have developed some long–term goals, pick one to focus on first and plan the steps you will need to reach it. Then you will work to complete these steps, one at a time. Each of these steps is called a "short-term goal." Choose one of the long-term goals you listed above and write it on the first line below. Then, list the steps or short–term goals you will need to reach on your way to achieving your long–term goal.

Long-Term Goal: _____

    Step 1: _____

    Step 2: _____

    Step 3: _____

    Other Steps? _____

More Challenging Goals

When planning a challenging goal, you may not be able to determine all the steps that you must take to achieve it. It is usually better to take more time to explore what makes it so challenging. Then, determine your first step and commit to a start date. One of the most difficult things to do in working toward a challenging goal is to take the first step.

Using the following three procedures, determine a goal and a first step, then commit to where and when you will take this first step.

1. On a separate piece of paper, write or draw something academically or personally that you would like to improve. (Some people express much more in a drawing.)

2. Decide on a "first step" you could take toward making the improvement. Write or draw yourself doing this step.

3. Commit to a day and time that you will take this "first step." Write this commitment in a goal statement. For example, "At 4:30 today, I will start my social studies homework."

Optional Activities

1. Talk about times each of you succeeded in reaching your goals.
    A. A success you remember having as a child.
    B. A success you have had more recently.
    C. A success you hope to have in the future.
Also discuss what is a success and what is a failure. Note that a failure to one might be a success to another person, and vice versa.

2. Keep a "Success Journal," which is a diary-like booklet in which you will write about your successes as you achieve them. You could include a list of some of your greatest successes in your Pilot Portfolio. Some things that might be included are:

    A. "A brief description of a success and what I did that helped me to succeed (try to use some of your own personal strength words)."
    B. "Something I learned about myself from this success."
    C. "How this successful experience felt to me."

LESSON 4. STUDY HABITS AND SKILLS

"Skill and confidence are an unconquered army."

George Herbert

If you would like to improve your grades in school, there are some tricks you can learn that will help you. These tricks are called "study habits and skills." Getting better grades may depend more on how well you use these skills than on how much time you spend studying.

James' Story

For years, James wished he could improve his school grades. Each time he received his report card, he was disappointed, but not surprised. His mother would say, "James, you have to study harder!" and James would start off each new grading period by doing just that. He studied very hard and did well for about two weeks. Then, he started putting off doing his homework and his grades started to slide once again. He became tired of trying so hard, and he began to watch more television and go out with his friends more often. Soon, he was failing many of his classes, and James became even more discouraged. Finally, James gave up trying because he didn't believe there was much hope.

This cycle is an easy one for students to slip into. Once you find yourself behind in your school work or become tired of trying so hard, it is easy to begin putting things off. It has been said that the difference between one letter grade and the one above it (for example the difference between a "C" and "B") only requires 5% more work. Why then do some students seem to get good grades while working so little to achieve them? One advantage they have is their confidence level. Other advantages are their study habits and skills.

Discussion Questions:

1. What are some reasons students your age put off doing schoolwork?

2. When have you ever felt like James? What did you do about it?

3. If you ever decide to encourage a younger student to study harder, how would you do it?

Keys to Becoming a Confident Learner

The following are strategies some students have used to become more confident about their abilities to succeed in school.

Key #1: **Set a few new goals at a time.** Review the previous lesson on goal setting.

Key #2: **See yourself being successful.** Picture in your mind what it will be like when you succeed at each of your goals. Remember to think of this picture whenever you begin to feel frustrated or discouraged.

Key #3: **Control your inner voice.** We all occasionally talk to ourselves in our minds. Unfortunately, some of the things we say to ourselves discourage us and make us want to put off or quit working so hard at something we need to do. Change these negative messages to more positive ones like the following:

Negative Self-Messages	**Positive Self-Messages**
• "I just can't do this work."	• "I can do this work."
• "I will never be able to do this."	• "I will be able to do this."
• "I will never be good at this."	• "I can keep improving."
• "I know I'm going to fail this."	• "I'm going to do my best."

Key #4: **Reward your accomplishments.** Once you have accomplished a short-term goal, give yourself a reward. Treat yourself to something special.

Key #5: **Encourage others.** Do you know someone who has become discouraged about school? When this happens, listen to his/her feelings. Then, offer some positive suggestions such as how he/she might find a tutor. When you help others to think more positively, it can have a positive effect on you, too.

30 Study Habits and Skills

Here is a list for you to look through and discuss with your Pilot. Begin by rating yourself on each of the items according to how well you use the strategy:

1 = Poor   *3* = So-So   *4* = Good
2 = Not so good   *5* = Excellent

Classroom Effectiveness

____**1. Keep Good Attendance:** Being in class is perhaps the most important thing you can do for your grades. When you miss a class, it usually takes twice the time to make up your work.

____**2. Set High Goals:** Write down what grades you hope to accomplish for each class and "aim high."

____**3. Show a Winning Attitude:** An important part of succeeding in a class is making sure your teacher sees that you care. Participate in class and avoid distractions.

____**4. Listen Carefully**: Pay close attention to the teacher. Sometimes, you can discover important hints about what to study by listening for emphasis in the teacher's voice.

____**5. Take Good Notes:** Take brief notes and emphasize the important points by underlining, highlighting, or using creative abbreviations.

Studying Reading Material

_____ **6. Use "SQ3R":** Survey, Question, Read, Review, and Recite. This is an old, but effective way to study reading material.

_____ **7. Skim the Chapter Questions First:** This will give you a feel for what is most important in the Chapter. Then look for answers to the questions as you read the Chapter more carefully.

Memorizing Facts

_____ **8. Use Acronyms:** Take the first letter of each term you want to memorize. Then make a nonsense word out of it. Or, you could create a new sentence with the same first letters for each word. For example, to memorize our solar system's planets in sequence from the sun, you can use the following statement: "My Very Excellent Mother Just Sat Upon Nine Pins." Another version for older students is, "Mary's Violet Eyes Made John Sit Up Nights Pondering" (Mercury, Venus, Earth, Mars, Jupiter, Saturn, Uranus, Neptune, and Pluto).

_____ **9. Use Word Associations:** Memorize a list of words that rhyme with each number 1-10. For example, one/run, two/shoe, three/tree, four/door, five/hive, six/sticks, seven/heaven, eight-/skate, nine/sign, and ten/hen. Then in sequence, picture each item you are trying to memorize with one of the rhyming terms.

_____ **10. Use "Rap":** Recite the terms or words you are trying to memorize with a rap rhythm. Rhythm can help you memorize much faster.

Writing a Term Paper or Project

_____ **11. Research:** Take the time to study your topic before you begin writing. Take brief notes and make sure you cite each source. This will help you relocate the information later if you need it.

_____ **12. Outline:** The key to an organized paper is a logical, clearly written outline.

____**13. Draft:** Don't worry about perfection here, just "get the words out." For example, it is sometimes better to avoid writing a paper in the order that it will finally appear. Start by writing the section that will be easiest for you.

____**14. Recast:** Once the first draft is completed, rework each section repeatedly.

____**15. Polish:** Check carefully the flow of what you have written and rewrite as needed for clarity.

____**16. Proofread:** Always double check your paper. Then have someone else double check it, especially for errors.

Taking a Test

____**17. Prepare:** Make sure you have enough time to study for a test. Sometimes it may help to have a study partner or team. Also, make sure you have enough sleep and eat a healthy breakfast before the test.

____**18. Reduce Stress:** Think of the test as a challenge and not a threat. If you are worried slow down; take a few slow, deep breaths; and make positive statements to yourself about how you are capable of succeeding on the test.

____**19. Become Motivated:** Remember that each test is important and don't give up. Give each question your best effort.

____**20. Be Test-Wise:** Make educated guesses and watch your pacing.

Studying Effectively at Home

____**21. Use your time wisely:** Don't spend too much time on one subject. When attempting to memorize, it is usually better to study in short 20 - 30 minute intervals with a brief break, than try to study for an hour or two, straight through. Perhaps, play "Beat the Clock" by guessing how long it will take you to complete the work you have in one subject. Then, time yourself and try to complete the work before that time elapses.

22. Set Goals: Set a goal each day before you begin working on your homework.

23. Prioritize: Decide which assignment is most important and do it first.

24. Prevent Distractions: You will accomplish more in less time if you do not have a television, stereo, or busy phone nearby. Find a place to study that is quiet, and comfortable. Some students, however, study better with soft music playing in the background.

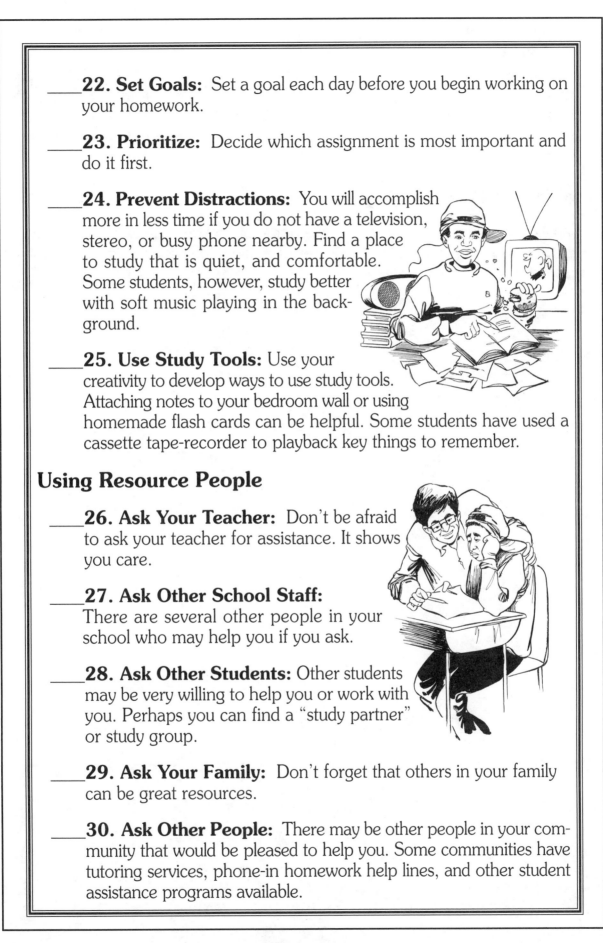

25. Use Study Tools: Use your creativity to develop ways to use study tools. Attaching notes to your bedroom wall or using homemade flash cards can be helpful. Some students have used a cassette tape-recorder to playback key things to remember.

Using Resource People

26. Ask Your Teacher: Don't be afraid to ask your teacher for assistance. It shows you care.

27. Ask Other School Staff: There are several other people in your school who may help you if you ask.

28. Ask Other Students: Other students may be very willing to help you or work with you. Perhaps you can find a "study partner" or study group.

29. Ask Your Family: Don't forget that others in your family can be great resources.

30. Ask Other People: There may be other people in your community that would be pleased to help you. Some communities have tutoring services, phone-in homework help lines, and other student assistance programs available.

Follow-Up

Look over any of the previous items that you marked "4" or "5" and recognize your strong points. Then, look at the items you marked "1" or "2" and set goals to improve in these areas. Select a strategy you will begin working on with your C-Pilot. Remember, "Your study skills are your school survival skills. . .use them wisely."

Optional Activity

Develop a weekly calendar showing your subject areas, assignments, tests, and short-term goals. Perhaps you can provide yourself with a reward each time you accomplish a goal.

LESSON 5: CAREER EXPLORATION

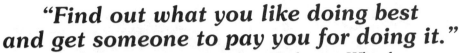

"Find out what you like doing best and get someone to pay you for doing it."

Katherine Whitehorn

Every teenager should start thinking about different possible careers. There are several factors that will influence your career decisions. Unfortunately, some people may try to discourage teens from believing they can reach their career dreams. Usually this is because the teenager's goals may seem unrealistic. But, don't lose sight of your dreams. There may be some goals that would be difficult for you to reach. But, if you have enough determination and are willing to make the necessary sacrifices and investments, you just might reach your dream career. On the next page is a list of some famous people who became very successful because of their determination and hard work.

Nine People Who Refused to be Discouraged

Thomas Edison was told by his teachers that he was too "stupid" to learn anything. Later, he repeatedly made more than 3,000 mistakes on his way to inventing the light bulb. Eventually he held 1,093 patents.

Wilma Randolph contracted polio and scarlet fever as a child and wore leg braces for nine years. She eventually became the first woman from the United States to win three Olympic gold medals in track and field.

Albert Einstein was four years old before he could speak and seven before he could read. One of his teachers described him as mentally slow, unsociable, and "adrift." He was later expelled from school. He is still considered to be one of the greatest physicists of all time.

Walt Disney was fired by a newspaper editor when he was young. He was told that he had "no creative ideas." His company's parks, movies, and other products touch the hearts of millions of people each year.

Michael Jordan was cut from his high school basketball team. Later, his accomplishments inspired several prominent sports writers to declare him the best pro-basketball player ever.

Oprah Winfrey suffered many drawbacks as a child because she was emotionally and physically abused. Yet, she became the first African American woman to host a nationally syndicated weekday talk show and to own her own television and film distribution company.

Bill Cosby became discouraged and dropped out of high school. He later received his doctorate degree in education and became one of the most successful entertainers and businessmen in the world.

Jim Carey also was a discouraged teenager. He dropped out of school in the ninth grade. His family was so poor they had to live in a camper and a tent. Later, he became the first comedian to earn twenty million dollars for appearing in a single film.

Agatha Christie had a writing disability so severe that she had to dictate her stories for others to type. Yet, she became one of the most famous writers of mystery novels.

What's Important to You?

The following are some of the reasons why people choose and enjoy certain careers over others. Select the three items that are the most important to you.

- ❑ Working with others in a team
- ❑ Working alone
- ❑ Working outdoors
- ❑ Being my own boss
- ❑ Receiving longer vacations
- ❑ Having flexible work hours
- ❑ Fixing or repairing things
- ❑ Creating or developing new things
- ❑ Working with computers
- ❑ Working at a job requiring physical strength
- ❑ Helping people or animals
- ❑ Playing a sport
- ❑ Entertaining others
- ❑ Traveling
- ❑ Selling things
- ❑ Helping people solve their problems
- ❑ Playing a musical instrument or singing
- ❑ Building things

10 Job Skills Employers Want to See

The following is a list of job skills that employers look for in new employees. Discuss how each of these "job skills" could be applied to different careers.

1. **Interpersonal Skills:** Be able to get along well with others.

2. **Reliability:** Show that you are a dependable person.

3. **Honesty:** Be trustworthy.

4. **Work Habits:** Be consistently responsible.

5. **Communication Skills:** Be able to write and speak effectively.

6. **Application Abilities:** Be able to apply knowledge to practical situations.

7. **Positive Attitude:** Be optimistic toward your job and employer.

8. **Persistence:** Be able to keep your efforts going.

9. **Flexible:** Be able to shift tasks easily.

10. **Resourceful:** Know when and where to find answers or ask for assistance.

Careers in My Family

Write the name of each of the following members of your family. Then list and tell about the type of job or career in which they have worked. Then, using the "10 Job Skills" on the previous page, write the numbers of the skills (1-10) that you think are the most important for each particular job. If you don't know the careers of some of these people, leave the space blank.

Mother:_____

Father:_____

Step-Parent or Guardian:_____

Grandparents:_____

Older Brothers or Sisters:_____

Aunts and Uncles:_____

Other Family Members:_____

Follow Up

1. Are you interested in one or more of the above listed careers? if so, which one(s)?

_____

2. If you don't have a special interest in your family's careers, write one or more careers that <u>are</u> interesting to you. Then, write the numbers of the skills that you think are most important for that career.

_____

3. What is the career of your Co-Pilot? What are the skills most important for his/her job?

_____

Optional Activities

1. Choose at least two careers that interest you the most. Add one or two careers that you are somewhat interested in. Then, go to the media center, career center, or guidance office and look up descriptions of those careers.

2. Find and interview one or more people who work in each of the careers you identified in #1.

3. Check with the vocational program that is affiliated with your school. See if there is a "Job Shadow" type program and volunteer to become involved in it. Perhaps your Co-Pilot can assist you with this.

92

LESSON 6: FAMILY

Family is "The we of me."
Carson McCullers

The word "family" is difficult to define. Some people think of a family as a group of people who are related to one another. Others view it as a group of people who are living together in the same home. Regardless of how you define family, it is a group of people who have a powerful influence on the life of each of its members.

Every family has its wonderful points and its difficulties. There are no families that are perfect and problem-free. Likewise, there are no families that are all bad.

Jose's Story

Jose was a friendly boy who was doing well in school. Others believed that he was very fortunate to have such a "good" family which didn't seem to have many problems. Some of the other students in his school were jealous of him, believing that he had it "so easy" in his life. But, these students didn't realize how difficult Jose's life was with his family.

One day, Jose came to school very quiet. Other people didn't notice much, but Jose didn't talk to anyone that day. A few students thought Jose was being rude and unfriendly when he didn't talk to them. Later, another boy thought Jose was staring at him and it made him very uncomfortable. He walked over and threatened Jose that he would make him sorry if didn't stop. Jose threw his books on the floor and left school.

The next day, another student found out that Jose's younger brother had runaway from home earlier in the week. In addition, his favorite uncle died about the same time.

Discussion Questions:

1. What do you think is the reason that Jose didn't tell anyone about what was happening in his family?

2. Why do some students have difficulty requesting help for their family problems?

3. What do you think are the most common problems that most families have?

4. What are the main reasons that a family is so important to each of its members?

My Family

Circle the number after each characteristic below that best describes how you and your family relate with one another.

1 = Almost never   **3** = Unsure   **4** = Some of the time
2 = Seldom   **5** = Almost always

Have fun together.	1	2	3	4	5
Help each other when there's a problem.	1	2	3	4	5
Communicate honestly and openly.	1	2	3	4	5
Make decisions that are fair to one another.	1	2	3	4	5
Understand each other.	1	2	3	4	5
Talk positively about each other.	1	2	3	4	5
Tell your true feelings to each other.	1	2	3	4	5
Spend enough time together.	1	2	3	4	5

Follow Up

If you answered most of these items with "1" or "2" it is possible that your family situation may also be having a negative effect on your school work and on your relationships with others. You may want to see someone else who understands and can offer support such as another relative or a counselor.

COUNSELOR

Family Influence

We are all influenced by our families. Whether we like it or not, the way we think, believe, act, and react are all affected by our families. Sometimes we may be surprised to discover that we act just like someone else in our family. What are some things you learned from your family that you will try to pass on to your own family someday?

Check the items below.

- ❑ Honesty
- ❑ Trustworthiness
- ❑ Patience
- ❑ Humor
- ❑ Pride
- ❑ Generosity
- ❑ Humbleness
- ❑ Good communication
- ❑ Positive attitude
- ❑ Belief in hard work
- ❑ Organization
- ❑ Fairness
- ❑ Friendliness
- ❑ Determination
- ❑ Kindness
- ❑ Respect
- ❑ Religion
- ❑ Appreciation for education
- ❑ Other

Optional Activity

On a large piece of paper, draw your family tree. Include both the mother's and father's sides of the family. Be sure to also include brothers/sisters, adoptive or step-parents, foster parents, guardians, and any other people living in your household. Don't worry if your "tree" ends up looking more like a bush because of all the current family members.

Once the family tree is as complete as you can make it, share with your Co-Pilot which people listed in your tree influence you the most in the items listed above.

LESSON 7: HEALTHY RELATIONSHIPS

"(A friend is) a present you give yourself."
Robert Louis Stevenson

Having different kinds of relationships with others provides you with many learning opportunities. Whenever you enter into new relationships, you will learn many new things about yourself and others. This learning process is important in preparing you for adulthood. But, some teenagers seem to keep finding themselves caught in relationships with controlling or abusive people. They may regret ever getting into these unhealthy relationships, yet they keep finding themselves back in them over and over again. Melissa is one of these people.

Melissa's Story

Melissa cannot understand why she always seems to find herself in relationships with guys who are very possessive and controlling. Looking back at the boyfriends she's had, each was very jealous and mean to her.

Melissa does not look for this kind of guy, yet she seems to be more attracted to those who criticize her. As each relationship becomes more negative, Melissa works very hard to save it. But this never seems to work very well.

Melissa's friends told her she needed to find a guy who would treat her with more respect. But Melissa would answer, "The ones that are nice and polite are so boring."

Now, Melissa is dating a guy who will not allow her to spend time alone with her friends. He tells her that where he goes, she goes. Every now and then Melissa sneaks some time with her friends, but she is worried he will find out. Although she is not happy in this relationship, Melissa says she can't tell her boyfriend about her real feelings or he will surely break up with her.

Discussion Questions:

Melissa is an example of someone who repeatedly finds herself in the same kind of unhealthy relationship. Discuss your answers to the following questions:

1. What is unhealthy about this relationship?
2. Why do you think Melissa finds herself attracted to this type of guy?
3. What could Melissa do differently to prevent herself from being in this kind of relationship?
4. In your own relationship(s) with others, how can you reduce the risks of:

- Being with someone too possessive or controlling?

- Being too dependent on the other person?

- Being with someone who will be a negative influence on you?

- Pregnancy?

- Sexually-transmitted diseases?

- Being deeply hurt?

Unhealthy Relationships

The following list contains characteristics of unhealthy relationships. Check those items that apply to one or more of your relationships or to relationships between other people you know.

❑ Dominating/Controlling

❑ Dishonesty

❑ Rushed intimacy

❑ Poor communication

❑ One-sided attraction

❑ Big differences between the people

❑ Arguing too frequently

❑ Physical abuse

❑ Emotional abuse

❑ Use of alcohol and/or other drugs

❑ Interference by family or friends

❑ Flirting with others

❑ Rescuer (When one person keeps seeking troubled partners to "help")

❑ Troubled companions (When both partners have problems and their relationship is built on trying to rescue each other)

Developing a Healthy Relationship

Here are some ways to increase the chances of getting into a healthy relationship with someone. Discuss each with your Co-Pilot.

☞ Start the relationship slowly by having fun and getting to know each other. Talk with each other about your interests, strengths, goals, families, hopes, and fears.

☞ Plan to do a variety of activities together that could decrease the chances of being placed in an uncomfortable situation.

☞ Communicate your feelings openly about what you are and are not looking for in a relationship.

☞ Take turns sharing your personal beliefs and values.

☞ Don't be too pushy or too weak. Stand up for your rights, but don't become over critical of the other person.

☞ It has been said that the key to a healthy relationship is for each person to consistently show four characteristics: caring, accepting, understanding, and trustworthiness.

☞ If you have already experienced several unhealthy relationships or continue to be attracted to the same kinds of troubled people, see a counselor. Through counseling you may be able to discover how you can find happier and healthier relationships.

What do You Look For?

The following list of qualities are what some people your age look for in a relationship. Score each of the following items according to how important it is to you when you are considering a relationship. Discuss your responses with your Co-Pilot.

1 = Unimportant   2 = A little important   3 = Very important

___ Good looking
___ A nice car
___ Well dressed
___ Popular
___ Wealthy
___ Humorous
___ Respectful
___ Quiet or shy
___ Career minded
___ Honest
___ Muscular
___ Intelligent
___ Reliable

___ Sexually experienced
___ Sexually abstinent
___ Religious
___ Athletic
___ A close friend
___ Responsible
___ Interested in similar things
___ Outspoken
___ Good listener
___ Older than me
___ Younger than me
___ Adventurous
___ (Other)

Optional Activities

1. Think about a healthy relationship between two people that you've known. Discuss what they did that helped their relationship succeed? Then, think about an unhealthy relationship you have seen. Discuss what hurt their relationship?

2. Interview a counselor or pastor, and ask what he/she believes are qualities of a healthy relationship.

LESSON 8: PEER PRESSURE

"Learn to navigate your own course.."

Anonymous

Being accepted by peers is very important to most young people. This need for acceptance comes from a basic human need to feel like you belong to some kind of group. Sometimes, to become part of a group, we feel that we should dress like them and do things like them. This may be okay in some groups. However, the need to belong can also influence a teenager to do dangerous, illegal, and/or other negative things.

It would be best if every person your age would carefully select only positive and encouraging friends who avoid getting into trouble. However, this is not the "real world." Consider what happened to Mark in the following story.

Mark's Story

Mark was a new student at school. At the end of his first week, some other students approached him and were very friendly. Later, they asked if he wanted to hang out with them that evening.

Mark wanted to be liked by other students, so he agreed without hesitation. They met in front of the local movie theater and stood there for an hour. Then, one of the boys' brothers picked them up in his car and took them to someone's home. As they entered the house, one of the boys said, "Let's party! My parents are gone for the weekend."

The older brother brought in a case of beer and each of the boys grabbed a can, including Mark. Although Mark was uncomfortable with the situation, he didn't want to be different from the others. Later that evening, the boys were shocked when the parents walked through the door and caught them drinking. It was Mark's first week in the new school and already, he was in trouble.

Discussion Questions:

1. What were some of the risks involved in this particular group of friends?

2. How could Mark have avoided getting into trouble?

3. What else could Mark have done to find friends?

4. When have you felt pressured to do something negative with others your age?

Negative Peer Pressure

Check the things below that you have felt pressure from your peers to do.

- ❑ Cut classes
- ❑ Skip school
- ❑ Smoke cigarettes
- ❑ Use alcohol
- ❑ Use other drugs
- ❑ Steal
- ❑ Damage or destroy property
- ❑ Have sex
- ❑ Sneak out of your home
- ❑ Run away
- ❑ Cheat on school work
- ❑ Act up in class
- ❑ Be dishonest about something you did
- ❑ Fight
- ❑ Pick on someone
- ❑ Get revenge against someone
- ❑ Join a gang
- ❑ Be prejudiced
- ❑ Say you like something that you don't
- ❑ Be different from who you really are
- ❑ Do something daring to "prove" yourself

Positive Peer Pressure

People can also pressure someone to do positive things in his/her life. For example, check the following positive things below that you have felt pressured to do, or tried to get others to do.

❑ Try out for a sport

❑ Improve your appearance

❑ Avoid peers who are bad influences

❑ Change a bad decision into a better one

❑ Be honest about something you did

❑ Join a club or organization

❑ Listen to a different kind of music

❑ Stay out of trouble at school

❑ Try something new that is positive

❑ Do better with your schoolwork

❑ Avoid smoking cigarettes

❑ Avoid drinking alcohol

❑ Avoid drinking and driving

❑ Avoid using illegal drugs

❑ Start a musical group

❑ Abstain from sex

❑ Stay in school

❑ Help someone

❑ Make career choices

❑ Be yourself

❑ Avoid being prejudiced

Optional Activity

Circle of Friends: On a sheet of paper, draw a diagram similar to the one that appears below. This is your "Circle of Friends."

In the circle nearest to "ME," write the names of your closest friends. In the next circle, write names of other people who are friends, but are less close. Then, in the outer circle, write some names of people who you know, but you don't "hang out" with.

Discuss how you would avoid negative pressure if it came from any of the different people in your diagram. Then, talk about how you might use positive peer pressure to help some of these people if they were heading for trouble.

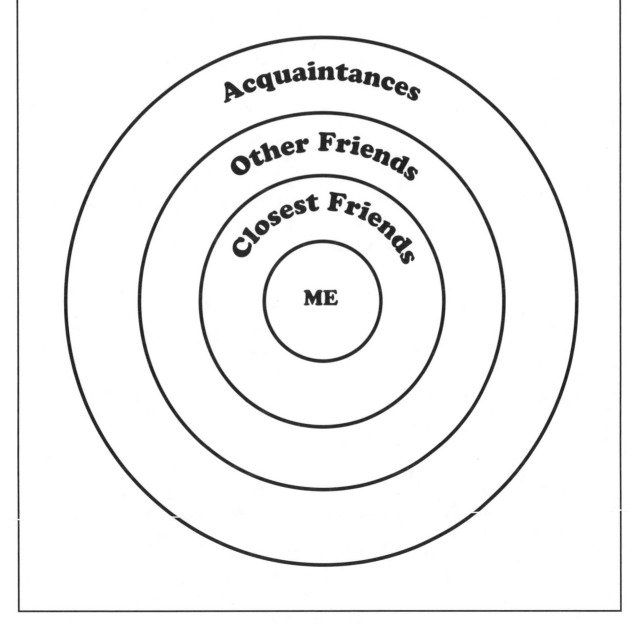

LESSON 9: STRESS

Stress is mental tension that causes several physical reactions. When we feel stress from fear, anger, or other feelings, our bodies prepare for "fight or flight." This means that we prepare to confront or get away from what is causing us to be upset. Our bodies do this by increasing our heart rate, blood pressure, breathing, and other physical responses. Once we deal with what is causing the stress, then these physical reactions slow down and we can relax again. However, if we can't or don't take care of the cause of our stress, then we remain tense.

When held for too long, stress can cause us to develop serious physical illnesses. For example, long-held tension is known to be one of the causes of ulcers, hypertension, asthma, hives, depression, and other illnesses. Long-term stress can also cause people to lose their abilities to think clearly and make good decisions. They may become depressed and need help from a professional doctor, psychologist, or counselor.

Tina's Story

Tina was a very hard working senior in high school. Each year she had taken the most difficult classes and received all A's on her report cards. She always expected herself to do better than other students. As a result, Tina didn't take time for friends. During her evenings and weekends and even during lunch, she would find a quiet place to study.

In the spring of her senior year, Tina was diagnosed with mononucleosis (Mono) and had to miss several weeks of school. Though she tried to do her schoolwork at home, she was not able to keep up with all the assignments in one of her subjects. As a result, Tina's situation became increasingly stressful to her. Near the end of the semester, Tina found that her grades had dropped. She felt that her situation had finally become hopeless. To everyone's surprise, she took an overdose of pills, attempting to commit suicide. Fortunately, she did not die.

When she was released from the hospital, Tina started meeting with a counselor. She discovered that she needed to work on how she could feel better about herself and better handle the stress in her life.

Discussion Questions:

1. Was there ever a time when you felt discouraged like Tina? How did you deal with it?

2. What are some positive things Tina could have done instead of trying to hurt herself?

3. What could you do if you noticed a student like Tina in your school?

Stress Test

In learning to handle your stress, it is important to check out how much tension you have at any given time. The following "Stress Test" will help you determine how much stress you are experiencing now. Check each of the following situations that are causing you stress in your life.

- ❏ Death of a relative or friend
- ❏ Pregnancy
- ❏ Troubles with rules or laws
- ❏ Dropping out of school
- ❏ Moved to a new home
- ❏ Fears about your future
- ❏ High expectations of yourself
- ❏ Disappointing grades
- ❏ Feeling pressured to succeed
- ❏ Feeling unsafe at school
- ❏ Boyfriend/girlfriend situations
- ❏ Relative or friend moved away
- ❏ Feeling unsafe outside of school
- ❏ Your friends or lack of them
- ❏ Upset at others your age
- ❏ Transportation difficulties
- ❏ Fears about your health
- ❏ Financial trouble
- ❏ Family problems
- ❏ Loss of a pet
- ❏ New job
- ❏ Leaving home
- ❏ Other problems

Just looking at the number of items you checked is not a good indicator of how much stress you have. Experiencing even a few of these situations could be the cause of a great amount of stress. Look through the items you checked and circle any that you believe are causing you the greatest amount of stress stress. Once you've finished, talk with your Co-Pilot about how much stress you have. Then, continue to the next page to explore ways of coping with your stress.

Learning to Cope With Stress

When we experience a lot of stress in our lives, we must find positive ways to cope with it. People seem to get themselves in the most troublesome situations when they use unhealthy ways of coping with their stress. Learning to cope in healthy ways with stress is one key to success in life.

The following list describes healthy and unhealthy ways of coping with stress. Put checks next to the approaches that best fit your style of coping. Then, discuss the long-term effects of each approach you checked.

Healthy Coping

❏ Writing out a positive step-by-step plan
❏ Taking care of your health
❏ Doing something helpful for someone else
❏ Talking about it with a friend, or family member
❏ Going to a counselor or other professional helper
❏ Doing something active
❏ Taking time to relax
❏ Using humor
❏ Directing your attention to something constructive
❏ Using your faith (for example, praying)
❏ Playing a musical instrument

Unhealthy Coping

❏ Eating too much (or too little)
❏ Taking it out on someone (or something) else
❏ Refusing to talk about it with others
❏ Avoiding (running away or escaping)
❏ Oversleeping
❏ Using alcohol/drugs
❏ Smoking
❏ Making excuses
❏ Denying a problem exists
❏ Hurting yourself physically
(or thinking about it)

Using Self-Talk

When you are under a lot of stress, it may help to say something to yourself that will calm you down a little. The following are some self-talk statements that can help.

➪ "I will learn from this situation and will be a better person because of it."

➪ "I know someone who will listen to me and understand my feelings."

➪ "Don't sweat the small stuff. . . and this is small stuff, really."

➪ "There are no failures, only different degrees of success."

➪ "In the long run, is this going to be really important?"

➪ "This situation is not a problem, it is an opportunity."

➪ "This situation is not a difficulty, it is a challenge."

➪ "I can remain calm with this difficult person."

➪ "No matter what happens, I will be okay."

➪ "I can bear anything for awhile."

➪ "I am a worthwhile person!"

➪ "I am doing the best I can."

➪ "This, too, shall pass."

➪ "I am true to myself."

➪ "One step at a time."

Optional Activities

1. Start with a deflated balloon. This is like a day without much stress. Describe little events that can cause stress to build such as oversleeping, forgetting about a test, and being accused of something you didn't do. After each story, blow more air into the balloon. Then, tell about some things you can do to help relieve stress. After each coping method, release some air from the balloon. Talk about how stress can be like this.

2. Interview people in particularly stressful jobs and ask them how they manage their stress. For example, seek out people who are in one of the following careers: police, medical professional, principal, teacher, coach, social worker, air traffic controller, or postal worker.

3. Write down one or more things that are causing you the most stress. Then attach the list to a helium balloon and release it. Or make a small "coffin" and have a stress funeral.

LESSON 10: ALCOHOL

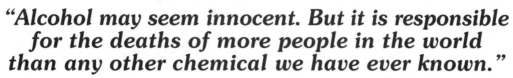

"Alcohol may seem innocent. But it is responsible for the deaths of more people in the world than any other chemical we have ever known."

Anonymous

The lesson to be learned from the abuse of alcohol is a tragic and continuing one. Using alcohol may seem like fun at first. But, there is always a price that must be paid for drug use and this price can sometimes be fatal.

Larry's Story

Larry was a 10th grader who received high grades in school. The day before Memorial Day weekend, Larry was asked by friends to go to a party. They told him that several of his friends would be there.

At the party, there were many people who were drinking alcohol. Some of Larry's friends talked him into playing a drinking game. They gave him a half-pint of 150 proof rum and asked if he could drink it down without stopping. As he drank it, others cheered him on. The next day, a newspaper article reported that Larry had died. The doctor said he died from acute alcohol toxicity.

Larry and his friends appeared to be very smart in school. They each did well with their school work. But he and the others at the party weren't very intelligent about the drinking of alcohol. Peer pressure, ignorance about consumption of high-proof alcohol and poor judgement caused Larry's death.

Discussion Questions:
1. What do you believe were the main reasons that people at the party wanted Larry to drink the rum?

2. Why do you think Larry agreed to play the drinking game?

3. If you were at the party, what could you have done to help, before Larry started to drink the rum? While he was drinking it? After he drank it?

Reasons Teens Give for Drinking Alcohol

The following are reasons why some teens say they drink alcohol. Check the ones you feel are the actual reasons why they drink.

❑ They are curious about what will happen.

❑ There's nothing else they can think of to do.

❑ It looks cool on TV or in the movies.

❑ They want to feel accepted by others.

❑ They want to forget their problems.

❑ It helps them to socialize.

❑ They like how it tastes.

❑ It quenches their thirst.

❑ Their parents drink.

❑ Their friends drink.

❑ To act grown up.

❑ It is hereditary.

❑ It helps them relax.

❑ They want to have fun.

❑ They want to live dangerously.

❑ They think it will make them "cool."

❑ Because of commercials about alcohol.

❑ They are rebelling against their parents.

❑ They want to attract someone they like.

© Youthlight, Inc.

Reasons for Not Drinking Alcohol

The following are reasons that teens your age should not drink alcohol. Check the ones that you feel are the best reasons.

- ❑ It can make you throw up.

- ❑ You may end up doing things that you regret.

- ❑ It is illegal and you may get caught.

- ❑ It can cause you problems at school and at home.

- ❑ It can result in a terrible hangover.

- ❑ It can keep you from having fun in other ways.

- ❑ Drinking too much alcohol can kill you.

- ❑ It can make you even more angry or very sad.

- ❑ It can cause you to not care about yourself.

- ❑ You can end up in a dangerous situation.

- ❑ It is addictive and can be difficult to quit.

- ❑ Sooner or later, it can kill you.

- ❑ It can hurt your relationships with people in your family.

- ❑ You can lose respect from others your age.

- ❑ You can be taken advantage of in different ways.

- ❑ It can make you lazy.

- ❑ When you have a job, it can cause you to be fired.

- ❑ It makes you act like somebody that you are not.

Facts about Drinking Alcohol

Test your knowledge about alcohol and other drugs on the following statements. Write a "T" or "F" in the space before each item to indicate whether you believe the statement is true or false. Then, compare your answers to those on the next page.

___ 1. Wine coolers have less alcohol than beer.

___ 2. You can become addicted to beer.

___ 3. Alcohol can increase someone's sex drive.

___ 4. Alcohol use is one of the primary factors in the deaths of teenagers.

___ 5. Teens say that their number one reason for drinking is because their friends do.

___ 6. Drinking alcohol is not as bad as doing drugs.

___ 7. Girls are slightly more affected by alcohol than boys.

___ 8. Alcohol is currently the second biggest drug abuse problem among teens.

___ 9. If someone is drunk and passes out, others should make sure the person is laying on his/her back.

___ 10. You can inherit from your parents a tendency to become an alcoholic.

___ 11. If a pregnant girl drinks only three beers, it won't cause severe birth defects in her unborn child.

___ 12. Having only one beer won't hurt your ability to drive.

___ 13. Excessive use of alcohol can damage your liver and lead to a deadly liver disease.

___ 14. Most teens in the U.S. do not try alcohol for the first time until after they are 15 years old.

___ 15. Most drowning victims have been drinking.

Answers

1. (False) Wine coolers typically contain 6% alcohol, while beer usually has 4% alcohol.

2. (True) Drinking beer excessively can lead to alcoholism.

3. (False) Alcohol does not increase sex drive. In fact, it reduces one's desire for and ability to have sex.

4. (True) Most deaths of teenagers have been related to drinking alcohol, whether these deaths are car accidents, falling, or other causes.

5. (True) According to one survey, seventy percent of teenagers say that their main reason for drinking is the influence of friends.

6. (False) Alcohol is a drug and is responsible for more deaths than the use of other drugs in the United States.

7. (True) In their digestive systems, females have lower amounts of an enzyme that breaks down some of the alcohol before it enters the bloodstream.

8. (False Alcohol is currently the most significant substance abuse problem among adolescents.

9. (False) If someone passes out on their back, they should be rolled over on their side. Too many people have died from breathing their own vomit into their lungs. This is how Jimmy Hendrix, the famous rock guitar player, died.

10. (True) Alcoholism has been shown to have a genetic factor.

11. (False) While this may not harm the child, then again, it may. Fetal alcohol syndrome is caused by the mother drinking alcohol while she's pregnant. The exact amount of alcohol it takes to harm the unborn child is unknown.

12. (False) Any amount of alcohol will slow your ability to make judgments and react. If you drive, don't drink! If you drink, don't drive!

13. (True) Your liver primarily serves to neutralize, or detoxify any chemicals in the body that it identifies as poisonous. Alcohol is one of these chemicals. Excessive drinking over a long period of time eventually will lead to a deadly disease called cirrhosis of the liver. Some alcoholics, even knowing that their livers are diseased, continue to drink until they die.

14. (False) In one survey, more than 60% of 15 year-olds report that they have consumed alcohol in the past.

15. (True) Of all drowning victims in the U.S., about 70% had been drinking alcohol at the time.

LESSON 11: OTHER DRUGS

"Drugs lie! They promise you happiness, and then they let you down."
Anonymous

Alcohol and other drugs are being used by an increasing number of young people. Some students begin using drugs when they are in elementary school. Using a drug is never worth the risks involved. Drugs may seem like fun at first, but one day an unexpected problem will strike. Whether it's becoming ill, getting busted and going to jail, losing a boy or girlfriend, getting fired from a good job, being robbed or assaulted, becoming hospitalized, or dying, the eventual results of drug use are always bad and never worth taking the risk that they won't result in tragedy.

Lisa's Story

Lisa was a ninth grader who spent most of her time after school with three close friends. One day two boys walked up to Lisa and her friends and started talking with them. Lisa was very attracted to one of the boys, but tried not to let him know.

Soon, the boy who Lisa thought was good looking took out of his pocket a bag containing what looked like a drug. He asked the girls if they wanted to try it. Lisa said "no" at first, but one of her friends said that she had done this kind of drug plenty of times before and that is was "cool." Strangely, this girl did not want to do the drug this time, but persuaded Lisa to try it.

The boy gave Lisa the drug. At first, Lisa felt a little dizzy. Soon, her heart started beating very fast and she began breathing quickly. But the boys told her not to worry and said that this effect was expected. Then Lisa suddenly passed out on the ground. One boy asked the other, "Where did you get that stuff?" The other boy answered, "I found it in my brother's drawer at home." Both boys looked at each other, then they took off running, leaving Lisa's "friends" to figure out what to do next.

Discussion Questions:

1. What do you believe are the reasons that Lisa tried the drug?

2. Why did one of her friends say that she had already tried the drug and that it was "cool"? Do you believe she had actually tried it before? If not, why would she lie?

3. What do you think the so-called "drug" might really have been?

4. What should her friends have done before Lisa took the drug? What should they have done after Lisa passed out?

5. What do you think should happen to the two boys?

Observations of Drug Use

Check which of the following statements are true.

❑ I have seen someone intoxicated or stoned on a drug other than alcohol.
❑ I have been offered drugs by someone.
❑ I know someone who has a problem with drugs.
❑ I know where I could get drugs.
❑ I have used one or more drugs in the past.
❑ I have seen someone use:

❑ Marijuana
❑ Alcohol
❑ Caffeine
❑ Tobacco
❑ LSD
❑ Cocaine
❑ Speed
❑ Ecstasy

❑ Heroin
❑ 'Shrooms (psychedelic mushrooms)
❑ Angel Dust (PCP)
❑ Downers (barbiturates/tranquilizers)
❑ Steroids (for body building)
❑ Inhalants (like gasoline or glue)
❑ Other drugs:

_____

Discussion Questions:

1 Which of these drugs are you unfamiliar with? Look them up in a book, or ask a counselor or nurse.

2. Which drug do you believe is the first one most kids experience before try others on the list?

3. Which three drugs on the list do you believe are the most dangerous?

4. Which three do you believe are the least dangerous? Talk about how these drugs are dangerous anyway.

5. Have you ever lost a friendship because of drugs?

6. Have you ever known someone who died, or almost died, while using drugs? What happened?

7. Have you ever known someone who committed a crime while intoxicated or high?

8. Have you ever known someone who needed help for their drug use, but did not get it?

Fun Without Drugs

Some adults believe that the main reason teens begin using drugs is because someone pushes them into it. However, interviews with young people indicate that the primary reason adolescents use drugs is because they believe that becoming intoxicated or high will be "fun." While having fun is an important part of life, there are many other ways to have fun that are much safer and don't make you sick afterwards.

If someone is going to promise never to use drugs, he/she will need to know many ways to have natural fun without the use of chemical intoxicants. Place a check mark in front of the following things you could enjoy doing without drugs.

❑ Play team sports such as baseball, basketball, soccer, football or hockey.

❑ Play any of the above sports without being on a formal team.

❑ Play games such as pool, chess, checkers, cards, video games, or board games.

❑ Go bowling with some friends.

❑ Go skating or skate boarding with friends.

❑ Go snow skiing or sledding with friends.

❑ Go swimming or boating with friends.

❑ Learn to play a musical instrument.

❑ Listen to music alone or with friends.

❑ Go dancing.

❑ Write poetry, music, and/or lyrics.

❑ Create something with arts or crafts.

❑ Get involved in one or more interest clubs.

❑ Take up martial arts.

❑ Hang out only with friends who are drug free.

❑ Go to the shopping mall.

❑ Go camping or hiking.

❑ Plan a drug-free event in your neighborhood.

❑ Plan a trip with your friends.

❑ Go biking.

❑ Go to a local recreational facility.

❑ Go to drug/alcohol free parties.

❑ Take up a hobby such as collecting something.

❑ Watch television.

❑ Go to the movies.

❑ Learn to cook.

❑ Go watch a sport's team practice or play.

❑ Go to a park with some friends.

❑ Mentor a young child.

A Message to a Child

If you were going to talk with an eight year-old child about drugs, what are three things you would say?

1.

2.

3.

Optional Activities

1. Interview a drug rehabilitation counselor. Beforehand, work with your Co-Pilot to make a list of interview questions.

2. Talk with your school's DARE Officer, if you have one, about the drug problem.

3. Make a list of drug free groups and events in your community in which you can get involved.

4. Work with your Co-Pilot and perhaps with others in your program to organize a drug-free event in your school or community.

LESSON 12: ANGER MANAGEMENT

"(Anger) starts with madness and ends with regret."
Abraham Hasdai

Anger is a normal human emotion that we should not try to eliminate from our lives. However, if we do not understand why we become angry and how we can manage it, difficulties result.

Anger is sometimes called a "secondary" emotion because we usually experience feelings of hurt, frustration, loss, or fear before anger develops. Think about which of these emotions might come first before you become angry in different situations. Remember that different people become angry about different things.

Allison's Story

Allison almost always had an angry look on her face. She knew she became angry a lot, but really didn't know why. She had been that way ever since she could remember. Allison was determined to never let anyone disrespect her without "paying a price." Unfortunately, it was Allison who usually ended up paying the price for her anger.

One day Allison had finally reached her limit with a girl at school who she claimed was telling lies about her. Allison was in a rage. She was so mad that she didn't think clearly. At the beginning of her lunch period, Allison found the girl and started hitting her without saying a word. Before the end of the day, Allison was suspended once again. The principal warned her that if she continued her violent behavior, she would be expelled from school.

When she returned to school, Allison met with a counselor who helped her finally discover the source of her anger. When she was three years--old her mother had died. Allison had made herself forget about the pain and grief from this horrible event. Because she had never really talked about this situation with someone, it continued to affect her life. Underneath, Allison remained angry that her mother had "left" her when she died.

Once Allison realized why she became angry so often, her counselor encouraged her to begin exploring different strategies she could use to help her get over her mother's death and control her anger. Allison still became angry sometimes, but she eventually learned to manage it much better.

Discussion Questions:

1. Why do you believe so many young people use fighting as a way to express anger?

2. What else could Allison have done when she was angry at the girl, that would have had a better outcome?

3. What would you have done if you were in a similar situation?

4. When have you felt hurt, frustration, loss, or fear before your anger developed?

What Makes you Angry?

Use the following numbers to rate how angry or frustrated you become in each situation below. Then share your answers with your Co-Pilot.

1 = No problem   **3** = Frustrated   **4** = Very Angry
2 = A Little Frustrated   **5** = Extremely Angry

How angry do you become when someone:

Promises to do a favor for you, then forgets.	1 2 3 4 5
Ignores you.	1 2 3 4 5
Blames you for something you didn't do.	1 2 3 4 5
Yells at you for doing something wrong.	1 2 3 4 5
Threatens to hurt you.	1 2 3 4 5
Starts a bad rumor about you.	1 2 3 4 5
Steals from you.	1 2 3 4 5
Tells you a lie.	1 2 3 4 5
Tells a lie about you.	1 2 3 4 5

Other *(List other situations that make you angry and rate yourself on each.)*

_____   1   2   3   4   5

_____   1   2   3   4   5

_____   1   2   3   4   5

Anger Control

The following lists provide some ideas for preventing or handling anger in positive and negative ways.

Directions: Check which of the following "Helpful" and "Unhelpful" ideas you use to control your anger. Then, discuss which of these ideas would be most appropriate for each situation from the previous page in "What Makes You Angry."

Helpful Ideas

❏ Talk it out with someone

❏ Count to "10"

❏ Take a deep breath

❏ Find a place to be alone

❏ Listen to music

❏ Punch a pillow

❏ Clean or organize your room

❏ Scream

❏ Walk, jog, or run

❏ Write it out

❏ Talk to yourself

❏ Play with clay or Play Doh®

❏ Draw your feelings

❏ Watch TV

❏ Go Shopping

❏ Play a sport

Unhelpful Ideas

❏ Eat a lot more (or less)

❏ Drive fast

❏ Use drugs/alcohol/inhalants

❏ Fight

❏ Threaten to hurt someone

❏ Hurt yourself

❏ Withdraw from everyone

❏ Blame it on someone else

❏ Take it out on an animal

❏ Destroy property

❏ Start a rumor

❏ Run away from home

❏ Skip class or school

❏ Laugh at the person

❏ Yell, cuss at the person

❏ Give an obscene gesture

Optional Activities

1. Look through a magazine or newspaper for examples of people who were angry. How did they deal with their anger?

2. Interview people in highly stressful jobs who have to deal with their anger. Ask them what they do to control their anger.

3. Visit a juvenile detention center.

4. Discuss the meaning of the following: "Anger is like a bomb. . .to make it safe, disarm its fuse."

LESSON 13: CONFLICT RESOLUTION

"You cannot shake hands with a clenched fist."
Indira Gandhi

Having conflicts with others is an inevitable part of life. Unless you choose to live the remainder of your life as a hermit, you will have to face occasional disputes with other people. Our successes or failures in handling these disputes depend in part on our mastery of skills and techniques of conflict resolution.

The Feud

Kelly and Tonya hated each other. But it wasn't always that way. When they were younger, the two girls were best friends. Then, during their eighth grade year, Tonya accused Kelly of "stealing" her boyfriend away from her. Years later, they continued to make little negative comments whenever they were around each other. A few times, these little comments caused one or the other girl to lose her temper and start fighting.

This year, each girl developed a group of her own supporters who would help spread rumors about the other girl. Eventually, some of these "friends" from each group began to threaten each other. Recently, even the girls' mothers have become upset at one another.

Kelly and Tonya spent a lot of their teenage years being upset at each other. <u>They</u> were the ultimate victims of this feud. Each of the girls suffered from negative rumors, stayed awake at night with anger and bitterness, and were eventually suspended from school for fighting.

Kelly's and Tonya's conflict was unfortunate. First, they probably could have resolved it long ago. Second, the conflict eventually took far too much of a toll on these girls, their friends, and their families. This entire situation should have been handled much differently by everyone involved. Discuss some ways the conflict might have been handled better.

Discussion Questions:

1. Have you ever experienced a feud with someone? How did it start? How did it end?

2. Why do you believe other people become involved so easily in a conflict between two people?

3. How could Kelly and Tonya have worked out their differences before the situation became out of control? What could they have done to help work things out later, after they were suspended from school?

4. What could the girls' friends do to help them work out their feud at this point in time?

5. Do you believe there are some conflicts in which fighting is the only way to work things out? Why or why not?

Handling Conflicts

There are many ways that people try to resolve conflicts. What are some of the advantages and disadvantages of the following ways?

- Yelling
- Ignoring
- Fighting
- Laughing at the person
- Talking about it with a friend
- Trying to forget about it
- Talking about it with a teacher, counselor, or parent
- Writing a letter to the person
- Spreading a rumor about the person
- Asking some friends to help you get revenge
- Trying to "talk it out" with the person in private
- Trying to "talk it out" with the person, in the presence of others

When you have conflicts with other people, how do you handle them? Discuss how you would probably handle the following situations:

- If someone cut in line in front of you.

- If your parent (guardian) told you that you couldn't do something you really wanted to do.

- If you found that one of your friends has been telling lies about you.

- If your teacher became upset with you in class.

- If someone threatened to fight you.

- If someone accused you of doing something that you didn't do.

Four-Step
Conflict Resolution Model

Sometimes, it seems like there are no good ways to resolve a conflict. When this happens, you will have to do the best you can in the situation. The following Conflict Resolution Model can help you make wiser decisions about how to handle your conflicts with others. It will provide you with a method that you can use with your parent(s), teachers, and others your age. You may also find that it can be used to help others work through some of their conflicts.

To build your skills in using this model, you may want to try out each step by role-playing some practice situations with your Co-Pilot. As you master the steps and learn how to apply them to a variety of situations, you will acquire some powerful tools to help you handle conflicts wisely.

Step 1: "What is the conflict about?"
Consider how the conflict started and try to think about both sides of the conflict as much as possible.

Step 2: "What approaches have you tried?"
Make a written list of all the approaches you've tried so far to resolve this conflict. After each item, write what happened as a result.

Step 3: "What else could you do?
Continue your list of approaches by adding any new ideas you may have to resolve this conflict. As in "Step 2", write what you believe will be the probable outcome or result of each strategy. If you cannot think of any new approaches, explore what would probably happen if you did nothing.

Step 4: "What's your first step?"
Look through your list of approaches and outcomes from Steps 2 and 3 and pick the one you will start with. Remember, if you decide to do none of the approaches, you still have made a choice that will have its own result. Commit to a day and time you will do this "first step." Then take action! Later, you may want to look back at your list to consider other ideas, in case the first step doesn't resolve the situation.

Optional Activities

1. Interview a professional mediator. You can find a list of these professionals in the Yellow Pages of your phone directory under a term similar to "Mediation Services," or contact your local courthouse for information.

2. Find out if your school or community has a peer mediation and/or a student court program. Volunteer to become involved in one of these programs.

3. Fill a small pan or plastic container half full of cornstarch paste. This is made by adding water to cornstarch powder slowly until a very thick paste results. Then place your fingers in the paste. You will notice that when you push hard against the paste, it will resist and feel like a solid. But, when you ease your fingers into the paste, the resistance disappears, allowing easy dipping. The point is that when attempting to resolve a personal conflict, a hurried, forceful approach usually causes resistance. On the other hand, a gentle, easy, and patient approach to conflict resolution will more likely result in discovering and working out the underlying issues.

© Youthlight, Inc.

LESSON 14: BEING ASSERTIVE

"One of the most important tasks teenagers have is to slowly and deliberately learn how to take charge of their own lives."

Anonymous

All of us become upset at times with things that others say or do. How we respond in these situations will tell others something about us. We don't want to respond too strongly or too weakly. When people upset us, we should try to be assertive. This means that we should be able to respectfully tell others about something they said or did that bothered us. When this happens, the statement we make to them is called a confrontation. All of us face, from time to time, situations in which we must confront others.

Nathan and Derek's Story

Nathan and Derek had many similar interests, but there was one primary difference between them. When Nathan felt the least bit upset about something, everyone around him soon knew about it. He was determined to stand up for himself and frequently confronted others in a very aggressive way. Nathan believed in being open and honest with his feelings. However, others sometimes avoided him because they felt he was insensitive and self-centered. They saw him as "too aggressive."

Derek, on the other hand, was shy and reserved. When he was upset at someone, he usually became quiet and walked away. He usually kept his true feelings hidden from others and rarely would confront someone. Derek believed in being very careful not to upset people's feelings. Because of Derek's nature, other students sometimes took advantage of him because they felt he was weak and wouldn't stand up to other people. They saw him as "too passive."

As a result of Nathan's aggressive style or Derek's passive nature, each boy had frequent problems with other students. They both would improve their relationships with others by learning how to be more assertive.

When confronting others, some people are too aggressive. This means that they are overly critical and harsh to others when they are upset. People eventually learn to avoid aggressive people because they don't like being treated so negatively.

Some people are too passive. This means they often avoid sharing their feelings when they are bothered by others. Passive people are sometimes taken advantage of and picked on by others.

Assertive people have a style that is between aggressive and passive. This is usually the most effective way to handle yourself when you need to confront others.

Discussion Questions:

1. Who do you know that is too passive? Too aggressive? What are the results of their styles of confrontation?

2. Who do you know that handles him/herself well when confronting others? When have you heard this person being assertive to someone?

3. Which style are you closest to: passive, assertive, or aggressive? What do you believe you need to work on to improve your ability to be more assertive?

Passive, Assertive, or Aggressive?

In the blanks that appear in front of the items listed below, use numbers 1, 2, or 3 to indicate whether this result would most likely be experienced by a student who is too passive, assertive, or too aggressive. Note that the answers are printed upside down at the bottom of this page.

1 = Too Passive (Usually trying to avoid expressing their feelings)

2 = Assertive (Carefully wording expressions of their feelings)

3 = Too Aggressive (Usually telling others in a strong, direct manner about their feelings, without trying to be tactful)

The student who is most likely to be:

_____ Suspended from school for fighting.

_____ Thought of as a "weak" person.

_____ Respected by others.

_____ Thought of as a rude person.

_____ Thought of as an effective leader.

_____ Picked on by others.

_____ Thought of as a strong, but caring person.

_____ Becoming ill someday, because of held-in feelings.

_____ Abusive to others.

Passive people need to build their confidence so they can confront others when needed. Aggressive people should practice being more sensitive to other's feelings when they become upset.

Good leaders have effective confrontation skills. They are not too harsh or too weak when they tell others how they feel. By practicing effective confrontations, you will learn an important leadership skill that will help you relate better with others throughout your life.

Answers: (1) 3; (2)1; (3)2; (4)3; (5)2; (6)1; (7)2; (8)1; (9)3.

Tips for Confronting Others

Remember, when deciding how to confront someone:

- **Choose your battles carefully.** That is, don't confront people each time you feel a little upset. Pick wisely which times you should confront a person, and which times you should let the situation pass by without saying anything.

- **Watch your timing.** It is sometimes best not to confront someone when you are very upset. Take some time to cool down and find the best words to say before you confront them

- **Use the "Three Step Confrontation Model."** This model can be helpful in planning how to give an effective confrontation (see next page).

- **Be prepared to be a good listener.** After giving your confrontation, you will need to listen carefully as the other person responds. Then, if you think that the person did not clearly understand what you were saying, tell the confrontation again.

Three Step Confrontation Model

This model will help you construct the most effective assertive statement you can give to others. When confronting others, try to use all three steps in any order.

Step 1: Tell the person specifically what he/she said or did.

Step 2: Tell the feeling you are experiencing.

Step 3: Explain how this feeling has affected you.

The following is an example of a confrontation using the three steps of the Confrontation Model. Look for each of the three steps in this statement.

> "I heard you telling Heather that I went out with her boyfriend. It made me mad because it's not true. I thought you were my friend, but now I'm not sure I can trust you."

On the lines that follow, write your own three step confrontation to someone who has said or done something that has upset you.

_____

_____

_____

_____

_____

_____

Optional Activities

1. Look for/or join a martial arts training program that features violence prevention and personal growth.

2. Practice role-playing situations you actually are facing.

LESSON 15: RACISM

"Racism will use any excuse to excuse itself."
Mary McLeod Bethune

Racism, like other forms of prejudice, is a prejudgment about someone based on a limited number of facts. For example, many people have experienced someone judging them based on, as Martin Luther King said, "the color of their skin, rather than on the content of their character."

Bessie Coleman's Story *

Ever since Bessie Coleman was a little girl, she dreamed of being a pilot. It was the early part of the 1900s and airplanes were a rare sight to behold.

In Bessie's childhood, life was not easy. She had to pick cotton to help support her family. When Bessie was in her 20's, she decided she was going to reach her dream of learning how to fly an airplane. She tried very hard to find a flight school that would give her lessons and she was turned down by every flight instructor she approached. Most of them were appalled that a woman would want to fly, especially a black woman! There were no African American pilots at that time.

After many failed attempts, Bessie finally found a flight school in France that would accept her. She worked hard at several jobs to earn the money for the trip and attended a "language school" to learn French. Then, she made her way to Europe. There she was licensed as a pilot, two years before Amelia Earhart had received her pilot license. After returning from France, Bessie became a stunt flyer and traveled across the United States.

Bessie Coleman was the first African American to earn an international pilot's license and the first black woman in the world to fly an airplane. Known later as "Queen Bess" she challenged racism and bigotry to reach her dream.

Though Bessie Coleman experienced racism in her quest to reach her dream, she did not let that get in her way. Like Bessie, many of us have experienced racism, or other forms of prejudice, and have overcome it. It would be best if no racism existed, but unfortunately, it does.

Discussion Questions:

1. How much racism do you believe is in your school? In your community?

2. What programs are in your school and/or community to help combat racism?

3. How might Bessie Coleman's life been different had she let racism discourage her from becoming a pilot?

4. When have you or someone you know experienced racism?

* Adapted from Rich (1993)

Experiences With Racism

Check the items in the list below, if you have ever experienced any of these situations involving racism. Discuss each situation, how you felt, and what you did about it.

I have been:

❑ Teased or laughed at.
❑ Discouraged from trying to do something.
❑ Talked about behind my back.
❑ Treated overly nice, without sincerity.
❑ Forbidden from going somewhere (or with someone).
❑ Denied admission into a club or other group.

❑ Ignored.
❑ Threatened.
❑ Held back from opportunities.
❑ Blamed for something that happened.

Origins of Racism

How do people develop racism? Check any items below that you believe are the origins of racism in people. Discuss which items you believe are the biggest causes of racism and why.

❑ Birth (genetic)
❑ Parent's beliefs
❑ Negative past experiences
❑ Fears
❑ Jealousy
❑ Organized groups
❑ Friends' beliefs

❑ Not being around people of other cultures
❑ Things that happened in past history
❑ Outspoken leaders
❑ Poverty
❑ Ignorance
❑ Media such as movies, television, and music
❑ Other _____

Doing Something About Racism

What can you do to help prevent or reduce racism? Look through the following list and check what you have done in your school and/or community. Then, place a star next to any item you would consider doing sometime during the next year.

___ Construct a bulletin board on "Cultural Unity."

___ Become a friend to someone of a different culture from you.

___ Start a multicultural study group.

___ Confront someone when they tell a racial joke.

___ Organize a multicultural event at your school.

___ Become a mentor to a child who is a different culture from you.

___ Reach out to a new student who is a different culture from you.

___ Write an article for your school newspaper on cultural diversity.

___ Organize a one-day conference for students on cultural unity.

___ Develop a multicultural theme skit or play for younger students.

Optional Activities

1. Go to the school media center or to a library and look up information about famous people who overcame or worked to reduce racism.

2. Look through magazines and/or newspapers and find examples of racial issues.

3. William A. Ward once said prejudice was, "A disease characterized by hardening of the categories." Discuss the meaning of this statement.

Three Co-Piloting Stories

1. *Anna's Story*

(Anna is a high school teacher)

At first, I was concerned about taking on another project with all my other commitments at school. But the Co-Piloting Coordinator encouraged me to become involved in this program because of my rapport with troubled students. Some of our more "at risk" students in the school seem to gravitate to me each year. However, I am not always sure how I can help them. By becoming a Co-Pilot, I have learned to understand and appreciate my natural talents as a helper to these students. I also benefited personally from working at the skills and activities in our Co-Pilot training program.

After our training, I was matched with Jenny, a 10th grader who was referred to the program because of her lack of self-confidence. When we were trying to decide on a mutual time to meet, I thought it might not be possible with our block scheduling. But some of her elective teachers cooperated and allowed her to miss some class time each week so that Jenny and I could meet during one of my planning periods. Her teachers allowed her to make up any work she missed. I also met with Jenny for one lunch period each week. Later, I found that we could also meet at other occasional moments during the week.

Initially, I wasn't sure what to do with such a shy, quiet person like Jenny. How could I connect with her? Eventually, we discovered that we both liked drama. We talked at length about several plays we saw, and I was careful to let her do most of the talking. I encouraged Jenny to try out for a role in the school play. She was surprised and excited when she found out she had been offered the role. Each week I helped her practice her lines. I was so proud when I watched her play her part with such assurance.

As we continued meeting, I felt a growing bond between Jenny and me. The next year, Jenny joined the Drama Club at our school. Interestingly, I felt a boost in my own self-confidence as Jenny increasingly risked trying new things. One time, she told me that she felt she could tell me "almost anything." What a compliment from a teenager!

Jenny continued to be my Pilot until she graduated from high school. Although I am no longer seeing her on a regular basis, I still receive letters from her telling me about life at her university. There is no better reward than to actually be able to see that you have helped make a positive difference in a young person's life.

2. Arthur's Story

(Arthur is a Loan Specialist working in a local bank)

When I realized all that was involved in the program, I almost backed out. I was told I would have to attend the Co-Pilot training, commit to at least one year, check on my student's school progress, etc. However, after talking with some others who were already Co-Pilots in the program, I decided to make the commitment. This was a decision I never regretted.

The Co-Piloting Coordinator matched me with Terrance, a 13 year–old with quite a negative reputation with teachers in his school. I learned that Terrance never knew his father. He also had school discipline problems and a brother who was serving time in prison. I realized that Terrance might be headed toward some serious troubles and thought that maybe a Co-Pilot could provide him with something he had never had in his life--a mentor.

My first meeting with Terrance was at the school and was set up by the Co-Pilot Program Coordinator. I used some of the Co-Piloting listening and affirmation skills I had learned in the Co-Piloting training. Our relationship really began when I asked him to help me improve in basketball. Terrance enjoyed showing me new moves and eventually I got to the point where I could give him a fairly good one-on-one game.

It was three weeks before Terrance indicated to me he had something more than basketball and casual talk to bring up in our meetings. My patience paid off when Terrance finally told me he could use help with some of his schoolwork. He explained that he was frequently frustrated and easily discouraged with his schoolwork. Of course, he placed most of the blame on his "unfair" teachers. I helped him set some new academic goals based on some of his own strengths.

With permission from Terrance and his mother, I found an academic tutor to meet with him on Mondays and Thursdays. Later, some of the other Co-Pilots and I brought our Pilots to a local park every week to play basketball. We also took our Pilots to ball games, on camping trips, and to other events, with their parents' permission, of course. Being a Co-Pilot with Terrance started as a one-year commitment. Now, I'm surprised that we are beginning our fourth year together. He is still struggling with some of his academic subjects, but he is hanging in there and hopes to go to college when he graduates. This year, Terrance volunteered to become a student Co-Pilot to a younger boy in elementary school. This boy reminds Terrance of himself at that age. Learning about this was perhaps the greatest reward I received from participating in this program.

3. Josh's Story

(Josh is a senior in an urban high school)

When I first found out that there was going to be a student Co-Pilot program in our school, I wanted to be in it. I had some troubles when I was growing up, and thought that maybe I could help a younger student who was having a hard time. The other student Co-Pilots and I went to a one-day training just before school started last fall. I was surprised how much I learned about being a more effective helper to someone. Practicing the different Co-Piloting skills was hard work, but it was very meaningful to me and the other students. We also had some fun together.

Once school started, I was matched with Chris who was a freshman. After Chris and I started meeting, it didn't take long before he was telling me about being very upset with his family situation. It bothered him a lot that he did not know his real Dad, especially when others talked about their fathers. I think what Chris needed most was a special friend to talk to about his real feelings. Most of what I did was listen to him and try to let him know he could tell me anything that was on his mind.

I really didn't give Chris much advice or try to solve his problems for him. He seemed to solve them himself when I sat back and really listened to and encouraged him. I don't think Chris had ever had someone to do that for him before.

Once during the fall, Chris seemed so depressed that I became a little worried about him. I talked him into meeting with one of the counselors, but he asked that I go with him to the first meeting. For the next few months, Chris met with the counselor each week and I kept meeting with him at other times.

Another thing that I think really helped Chris was the Strength Coaching activity we did together. This helped him learn that he had several abilities that he could use to make more friends and improve his school grades. Using this activity, I learned how to help him build more confidence in himself.

At the end of the school year, it meant a lot to me that Chris came to my graduation. I think this might have inspired him to stay in school and work hard to achieve his goals. Chris asked me to send him my address when I go to college next year. I plan to keep in touch with him.

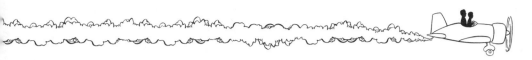

Bowman, R.P. (1997). *Study With a Buddy*. Chapin, SC: YouthLight, Inc. (In development).

Capuzzi, D. & Gross, D.R. (1989). *Youth At Risk: A Resource for Counselors, Teachers, and Parents*. Alexandria, VA: American Association for Counseling and Development.

Josephson Institute of Ethics (Dec., 1992). *Developing Moral Values in Youth. Ethics: Easier Said Than Done.* (Marina Del Rey, CA), Issues 19&20, 80-81.

Klots, S. (1995). *Carl Lewis Story*. New York: Chelsea House Publishers

Mosley, L.(1976). *Charles Lindbergh*. Garden City, New York: Doubleday.

Rich, D.L. (1993). *Queen Bess: Daredevil Aviator*. Washington, D.C.: Smithsonian Institute Press.